New Thought

New Thought

A PRACTICAL AMERICAN SPIRITUALITY

. . . . .

C. Alan Anderson
Deborah G. Whitehouse

CROSSROAD • NEW YORK

1995
The Crossroad Publishing Company
370 Lexington Avenue, New York, NY 10017

Printed in the United States of America

Library of Congress Cataloging-in-Publication Data

Anderson, C. Alan, 1930–
   New Thought : a practical American spirituality / C. Alan
Anderson, Deborah G. Whitehouse.
     p.   cm.
   Includes bibliographical references and index.
   ISBN 0-8245-1480-7
   1. New Thought. I. Whitehouse, Deborah. II. Title.
BF639A6778 1995
299′.93—dc20   94-47380
                                                           CIP

*

Acknowledgments

*P*ublisher Michael Leach of The Crossroad Publishing Company formed the basic idea of this book and suggested that we write it. In that sense, it is as much his brainchild as ours. His warm reception of what we have written and his helpful suggestions throughout the course of its writing have been invaluable. To him we offer our profound thanks.

This book is intended to be reader-friendly. To that end, we have omitted footnotes. However, it should be relatively easy (well, at least somewhat short of impossible) for the determined reader to locate the sources of quotations by using the bibliography, which includes sources of nearly all quotations used in the book. The bibliography also includes some other immediately relevant works that the reader may wish to consult.

All biblical quotations are from the Authorized Version of the Bible.

*

Contents

*

Preface

*T*his is a book about a distinctive yet typically American out-look—a practical yet spiritual way of life. It is written for people who know little or nothing about New Thought and for those who have been in New Thought for years without finding out much about what it is or its relationship to the larger spheres of religion and philosophy.

The book is intended to be both informative and inspirational, but inspirational in a way that is directly useful in the workaday world—useful with regard both to understanding and to application. Most New Thought books, largely self-help books, make no use of the term *New Thought* and ignore a comprehensive perspective in which New Thought is most fully understood. This book places New Thought and its applications in a philosophical and historical background.

Probably most Americans, if not most people in the world, accept large parts of New Thought teachings, although they may never have heard of New Thought by name. People may make such remarks as "It's all in your mind" or "If you believe you can, you can" (or its negative form, "If you believe you can't, you're right"), or even sing a bit of an old song that advises, "You've got to ac-centuate the positive, e-liminate the negative," without realizing that they are echoing teachings associated with New Thought. Many have heard of positive thinking or have even read the book *The Power of Positive Thinking* by the late Norman Vincent Peale, or listened to or read Robert Schuller on possibility thinking or power thinking, all without knowing

that they are absorbing New Thought a step or two away from
its direct expressions.

New Thought is a do-it-yourself religion or spirituality, in the
sense that you have to remake your own beliefs/attitudes/
expectations, to take responsibility for where you are now if you
are to be able to get to where you want to be in the future. But
to say *do-it-yourself* is not to say *do-it-by-yourself.* The prime belief
of New Thought is that God is here and is directly available for
anyone who chooses to cocreate constructively with him. So New
Thought is really an allow-God-to-do-it-with-you spirituality.

These days it seems as if almost everyone is something of a
do-it-yourself theologian. No longer are people likely to accept
any religion in toto; they pick and choose, accepting the parts
that seem helpful and rejecting the others. This is what New
Thought long has encouraged. This is not to say that it is because
of New Thought that people do this, just that New Thought
is typical of the American pick-choose-and-try-it-out attitude.
Perhaps this is at least partly because New Thought grew out
of the experiences of Americans who mostly had little formal
education, yet were not deterred in their work by either medicine or traditional religion. There is something of the Maine
woods and the frontier about New Thought, near enough to
conventional civilization to profit from it, yet far enough away
to ignore it with some ease. New Thought is unabashedly spiritual, but in a refreshingly this-worldly, here-and-now way; it loves
the divine enough to find God here, not just hereafter or in a
remote somewhere-up-there beyond understanding, if not beyond belief.

As the twentieth century is giving way to the twenty-first—
and many say that the modern age is being replaced by the
postmodern—there are so many physicists, physicians, seers,
gurus, and hangers-on singing songs of spirit-over-sense-
perception that it is difficult to get an accurate understanding of
the ideological landscape, to draw helpful lines of demarcation.
Clearly—or annoyingly unclearly—there is a convergence of
forward-looking thinkers and feelers, some from science and
others from a spirituality that partly lives in religions and partly
transcends them.

It is no wonder that New Thought no longer has such a distinctive place in the sun (or shade, depending on one's attitude) as it had a century ago. Some may wonder whether it still merits general interest. It does, partly because its very history deserves attention, but chiefly because it offers more clearly than does any other outlook a spiritual-practical path for moving beyond being stuck in one's troubles. It does this in a spiritual way, but not a superstitiously supernatural way.

New Thought has at least three aspects, and it can be entered through any of them. Like the blind men describing the elephant, some may think that it is one to the exclusion of the others. They are:

- *Psychological:* You get what you expect; your share of reality is what you believe it to be. New Thought is the reeducation of your expectation, not only intellectually, but at the heart of yourself. Unshakable certainty is the key to transformation. You are what you believe you are; you can change your beliefs and thereby change your world.
- *Metaphysical:* The basic nature of reality, of what God and you are and how the world works at bottom, especially in the healing of all sorts of situations.
- *Mystical:* The experience of unity with God, both for its own sake and for its usefulness as the foundation for one's practical transformation of living.

New Thought is simple enough to be practiced without much study, but open enough to allow for the greatest sophistication in development—even beyond the point that most people are likely to want to go at present. New Thought is still evolving; it may yet be the point at which religion, philosophy, and science come together as the most effective combination to move the world to greater peace, plenty, health, and harmony. It just might be the quintessential spirituality for the next millennium. At the 1994 International New Thought Alliance Expo, futurist Barbara Marx Hubbard predicted, "New Thought is now or will become in the next thirty to fifty years the most important single movement on earth."

Whether you accept New Thought or reject it, it is important for you to learn more about what New Thought is, where it came from, how it is evolving, and how to use it, if you wish. These topics are what this book is about.

1

✳

What Is New Thought?

A young woman dying of hereditary tuberculosis attends a lecture in 1886, leaning heavily on her husband's arm. He himself walks with a severe limp, having damaged his hip in a childhood skating accident that left him with a withered leg. The woman emerges from the lecture with a new and powerful belief: "I am a child of God and I do not inherit sickness."

Two years later, with no further medical intervention, the woman is completely well. Her husband's leg, no longer withered, has grown three inches longer, and the constant pain has disappeared. The husband and wife begin a ministry that becomes worldwide, healing and prospering many thousands of people.

An elderly Greek gentleman washes dishes in a hash joint, eking out a bare existence. He literally saves his pennies and invests them in thousands of shares of stock in the bankrupt Missouri Pacific Railroad, then selling for six cents a share. Each night, he writes out his vision for the railroad: new, enlightened leadership, new tracks and equipment, new prosperity. In the morning, he rereads what he has written and then burns the paper at the tiny sink in the corner of his shabby little room, "so that my words go forth into the universe." When a kindly stockbroker takes an interest in him, he explains that he is doing all this at the suggestion of his minister.

Months later, the stockbroker begins to read in the daily paper about the rebirth of the Missouri Pacific. First a line, then a column, then long articles describe the initial belief that it could be rebuilt, then the acquisition of intelligent new leadership, new track, and new rolling stock. Soon, Missouri Pacific is trading not for six cents but for $89 a share, and the astounded stockbroker is wracking his brain to recall the name of the elderly gentleman's minister!

The name of the minister was Ernest Holmes. The name of the lecturer was Eugene B. Weeks; his listeners were Myrtle and Charles Fillmore. All of them were students of Emma Curtis Hopkins, herself a student of a woman who had been healed by an unschooled Maine clockmaker and inventor named Phineas Parkhurst Quimby. Quimby believed that he had rediscovered the lost healing methods of Jesus. The loosely organized movement that began with him eventually became known as New Thought, and it consists of a number of independently developed branches such as Unity, Religious Science, and Divine Science.

Quimby never sought to found a new religion. He avoided both organized religion and organized medicine, turning, as did Jesus, to God as the Source of healing. Even today, New Thought embraces a minimalist creed, leaving the individual free to relate directly to God. It's a do-it-yourself religion. Its emphasis is not on *religiosity* but on *spirituality*.

Spirituality is perhaps the most important aspect of religion today. It refers, as religiosity cannot, to the intensely personal, devotional, life-transforming aspects of religion. It is a term preferred, for example, by people who have had enormously moving experiences but who are disinclined to engage in conventional religious alignments, activities, or orientations. Jesus said, "The letter killeth, but the spirit giveth life." Religiosity commonly is connected with the letter, the mechanistic, literal observance or prescribed practice of a system of beliefs.

Yet if New Thought is spiritual, it is also intensely practical. It is the application of one's religious beliefs to solve the problems of daily living. Originally dealing with problems of sickness, it rapidly expanded to include problems with lack of money or difficulties in relationships with other people. Jesus, in his great compassion for people, saw to it that their daily needs were met and taught us to pray for "our daily bread." The genius of New Thought is that, following the example of Jesus, it synthesizes the seeming opposites of practicality and spirituality. Yet New Thought goes beyond problem solving to teach us how to create the world we want by forming it with our thoughts. Jesus said, "I am come that they may have life and have it abundantly." New Thoughters believe in a life of abundance here and now.

American philosopher and pioneer psychologist William James referred to New Thought as "the religion of healthy-mindedness" and regarded it as the American people's "only decidedly original contribution to the systematic philosophy of life." Its principles underlie nearly all of the American success literature of the past century revealed by students of success from Orison Swett Marden to Napoleon Hill to Stephen Covey.

All the early leaders of New Thought came from Christian backgrounds, yet most of them had found organized religion restrictive or repressive and turned away from it. They were all deeply spiritual, though they were not all deeply religious. Since America was largely settled by people who came here to escape repressive religions, this should not be surprising. What is surprising is how often the oppressed become oppressors at the first opportunity. New Thought has happily escaped from that pattern, tolerating very great latitude in beliefs and practices. Yet critics have complained that New Thought did not insist on suffering as somehow necessary for salvation! The "religion of healthy-mindedness" has always been an upbeat, positive, optimistic way of life. Interestingly, recent research in psychology has revealed that optimists do better in every way, including health, longevity, and overall performance.

Not everyone in New Thought is seeking refuge from a religion that failed to meet his or her needs. Many people continue to be loyal members of a mainstream church while using New Thought as a little leaven for the loaf. The best-known example of this is the work of the late Norman Vincent Peale, a faithful Reformed Church minister who acknowledged in writing his debt to New Thought, the source of his Positive Thinking concept.

New Thought is what all Christianity could have become if it had been able to avoid the stultifying tendencies needed to compete with other outlooks for the title of official religion of the Roman Empire. It is what all Christianity could have become if it had allowed freedom of belief, concentrating on following the loving, healing example of Jesus rather than developing a rigid superstructure of teachings about Jesus.

What are the principles of New Thought, this peculiarly American philosophico-religious way of life? In a nutshell, New Thought is expressed in Romans 12:2, "Be ye transformed by the renewing of your mind." New Thoughters seek nothing less than total life transformation, empowerment through changing their thoughts and keeping them changed. The linchpin of New Thought is the Law of Mind Action: thoughts held in mind produce after their kind. There are many ways to express this: like attracts like; as in mind, so in manifestation; as in heaven, so on earth; "them that has, gets." This goes along with what philosophers refer to as *idealism,* belief that the world is really made up of thoughts or mind or spirit. Its opposite is *materialism,* belief that the world is made up of material "stuff" that one can measure.

In the long-standing battle between science and religion, idealists generally represented religion and materialists represented science. Ironically, physics, the king of sciences, the yardstick by which other sciences are measured, has now moved toward idealism with the discoveries of quantum physics. British scientist Sir James Jeans remarked that the universe looked like nothing so much as a giant thought. New Thought from its infancy has sought to bridge the gap between science and religion, and some of its branches have been given names such as Religious Science and Divine Science. Quimby studied mesmerism, or hypnotism, as did Freud later, because it was the latest scientific wrinkle of the day.

If this is a universe of thought, then changing one's thought changes the universe, at least a smidgen. Current physics teaches that the act of observing changes what is observed.

At the heart of New Thought is a minimalist creed, a simple system of beliefs that make optimistic idealism credible. As stated in the "Declaration of Principles" of the International New Thought Alliance, an umbrella organization for New Thought:

- We affirm the inseparable oneness of God and humankind, the realization of which comes through spiritual intuition, the implications of which are that we can reproduce the Divine perfection in our bodies, emotions and in all our external affairs.
- We affirm the freedom of each person in matters of belief.
- We affirm the Good to be supreme, universal and eternal.
- We affirm that the Kingdom of Heaven is within us, that we are one with the Father, that we should love one another and return good for evil.
- We affirm that we should heal the sick through prayer and that we should endeavor to manifest perfection "even as our Father in Heaven is perfect."
- We affirm our belief in God as the Universal Wisdom, Love, Life, Truth, Power, Peace, Plenty, Beauty and Joy, in whom we live and move and have our being.
- We affirm that our mental states are carried forward into manifestation and become our experience through the Creative Law of Cause and Effect.
- We affirm that the Divine Nature expressing Itself through us manifests Itself as health, supply, wisdom, love, life, truth, power, peace, beauty and joy.
- We affirm that we are invisible spiritual dwellers within human bodies continuing and unfolding as spiritual beings beyond the change called physical death.
- We affirm that the universe is the body of God, spiritual in essence, governed by God through laws which are spiritual in reality even when material in appearance.

Most mainstream churches would have little difficulty with these principles. New Thought believes that there is only one Power in the universe and that Power is good. New Thought at its most mature stage is *panentheistic,* meaning that all is *in God,* rather than *pantheistic,* meaning total identification of world and God, often with the idea that the world is illusion. One of us

(Alan) likes to say, "God is all there is and then some." New Thoughters often state that there is no place where God is not. "In him we live and move and have our being" (Acts 17:28). This means that we are all parts of God—more specifically, God's body—and there is God, the solution, at the heart of every problem.

> Whither shall I go from thy Spirit? or whither shall I flee from thy presence? If I ascend up into heaven, thou art there: if I make my bed in hell, behold, thou art there. If I take the wings of the morning, and dwell in the uttermost parts of the sea; even there shall thy hand lead me, and thy right hand shall hold me. If I say, Surely the darkness shall cover me; even the night shall be light about me. Yea, the darkness hideth not from thee; but the night shineth as the day: the darkness and the light are both alike to thee (Ps. 139:7–12).

No wonder New Thought is optimistic and upbeat!

Fundamentalists might have difficulty with the idea that the only Power in the universe is good. New Thought teaches that evil is insubstantial, that it is only immature or misused good. The devil is the invention of our minds, and goes as fast as he comes. When you walk into a dark room and turn on the light, the darkness vanishes; you don't have to chase it away. The Bible was written by Oriental minds for Oriental minds, and most of it was never intended to be taken literally. Jesus cast out demons, which is to say in the language of today that he straightened out people's thinking; our fear thoughts are demonic indeed.

But New Thought does not concern itself with most religious doctrines. If the virgin birth literally happened, wonderful; if it didn't, that's fine, too. And New Thought doesn't care what you do on Sunday morning. If you have a church that gives you spiritual food, great. If not, and you want some, New Thought has a wide variety for you to choose from, from banquets to picnics.

One special feature of New Thought, emphasized more in

some branches than in others, is known as *metaphysical interpretation* of the Bible. This misuse of the term *metaphysical* raises a few philosophical eyebrows, but what it really means is treating Scripture metaphorically or symbolically, seeking a deeper meaning beyond the literal. Jesus frequently taught in parables, which he later interpreted for his disciples. From the days of Philo Judaeus and of the early church in Alexandria, scholars have interpreted names in the Bible to arrive at deeper meanings. Charles Fillmore, cofounder of the branch of New Thought known as Unity, compiled his *Metaphysical Bible Dictionary* of these interpretations.

Some metaphorical interpretations are consistent throughout the Bible. This is truly remarkable when you consider that it was written at "divers times and in sundry places" by many different authors. For example, *man* and *woman* symbolize either body and soul or intellect and emotion. For this reason, well-meaning attempts to eliminate sexism in the Bible obscure deeper meanings. Unity minister Catherine Ponder and the late Divine Science minister Emmet Fox both have written extensively about metaphysical interpretation of the Bible.

Direct experience of God is sometimes called *mysticism*. It is associated with the right hemisphere of the brain and is frequently distrusted by logical thinkers, who are left-hemisphere dominant. But using only half a brain makes you a half-wit! We need a balance of mystical experience, sensory experience, and reason, all contributing to the "real world" of daily life. This is not a book on how to become a mystic, but it will acquaint you with one application of mysticism as a significant aspect of American spirituality. It will help you become more aware of what is going on around you, and—if you choose to put the information to work—will help you live life more effectively, with improved health, wealth, human relationships, and abundant happiness. Success can be defined as reaching reasonably challenging goals that you set for yourself. On that basis, New Thought is the royal road to success in life.

This book cannot tell you how to experience God directly— that is up to you and God—but it can give you a philosophical background for doing so, coupled with support based on scientific research to justify these beliefs. This is a thoroughly Western, American approach to spirituality, yet it is blessed and enriched with Eastern influence. Its roots are ancient, but its outlook is as new as tomorrow.

"One of the most significant findings in psychology in the last twenty years is that individuals can choose the way they think," writes experimental psychologist Martin Seligman. He was echoing William James, who wrote, "The greatest discovery of my generation is that a human being can alter his life by altering his attitude and mind." "As [a man] thinketh in his heart, so is he," wrote Solomon (Prov. 23:7). And Jesus said to the Roman centurion, "As thou hast believed, so be it done unto thee" (Matt. 8:13). It's aptly named—New Thought.

2

✳

Philosophical and Organizational Aspects of New Thought

*B*efore going into more detail about this remarkable way of life known as New Thought, we want to provide you with a setting: a philosophical, historical, and religious background against which to display New Thought. Like any other system of belief and action, New Thought did not spring up in a vacuum. There was a lot going on in thought, word, and deed in nineteenth-century American culture. Those goings-on produced P. P. Quimby and his followers. Philosophers call them *idealists,* and shortly we'll show you what that means and what other labels are available.

Since the days of the ancient Greeks, philosophers have been rumbling back and forth at each other about the basic nature of reality. Most of us don't lose much sleep over the issue because we don't see how it relates to our daily lives. Then when we get into a pickle, we frantically search for some understanding of what life is all about. But philosophy is an armchair enterprise pursued calmly and rationally outside of the fray. It's a dirty job, but somebody has to do it. You won't find many want ads for philosophers, and many philosophers have to moonlight, as did Stoic philosopher Marcus Aurelius, whose day job was Roman emperor. Still, philosophers do us the great service of systematically working out how the world has to be in order to be at all. This means that long before we get into difficulties, we can put our belief systems into place to help us get through them, or even avoid them altogether.

So let's humor the sages for a couple of pages before taking off on a brief gallop through history. It's philosophy made nearly painless, we promise, and it involves no heavy lifting.

Is There a Metaphysician in the House?

The endless rational search for the deepest level of truth is what philosophers call *metaphysics*. This is one of the most often misidentified or variously labeled birds in the linguistic woods. New Thoughters often refer to New Thought as *metaphysics* and to themselves at *metaphysicians*. This is disconcerting to anyone who is educated in philosophy. In that discipline, metaphysics is the branch that deals with the basic nature of all that is. The term goes back to Andronicus of Rhodes, who arranged the writings of Aristotle (382–322 B.C.) a few centuries after Aristotle's death. Andronicus put the writings that Aristotle called *First Philosophy* or *Theology* AFTER the writings on *physics*, hence *META*physics: *after* or *beyond* physics. So the term had a very prosaic original meaning. In the traditional sense, to call someone a metaphysician says that the person is interested in the topic of metaphysics. It does not tell us which beliefs about reality the person selects.

Many people use the term *metaphysics* to suggest attention exclusively to a realm beyond the physical, but metaphysicians traditionally have sought to understand that realm and the more familiar one by explanations that may or may not go beyond physics. Metaphysicians seek that which could not be otherwise, irrespective of whatever appearances it may take.

If metaphysicians believe that everything in the universe is really matter, they are called *materialists*. If they believe that everything in the universe is really mind or ideas, they are called *idealists*. If they believe that mind and matter are equally real, they are called *dualists* (and a few less complimentary things). Let us take a moment to look at these three categories, and then go on to notice whether philosophers in any category believe that the universe is static (the old view) or dynamic (the relatively new *process* view). Table 1, which is explained in the paragraphs that follow it, shows these competing positions in metaphysics.

Materialism. Materialism commonly means an orientation toward living that stresses attaining money and material things. It may imply crassness. The metaphysical materialist need not be like that, but in any case, believes that the underlying nature of everything is matter (or, in the updated version of materialism called *naturalism,* that everything is composed of lifeless energy). The materialist falls within the category of *monism* (one-ism) with respect to how many types of things make up everything, and with *pluralism* (more-than-one-ism) with regard to how many units of matter or energy there are. The currently most popular form of materialism explains everything in terms of various rates of vibration. An idealist might say that all vibration is an expression of mind, which itself is nonvibratory, being in the nature of thought and values, which are nonspatial. Process philosopher Charles Hartshorne defines materialism as "the denial that the most pervasive processes of nature involve any such psychical functions as sensing, feeling, remembering, desiring, or thinking."

Idealism, the Metaphysical Position of New Thought. Idealism commonly means high-mindedness, even unrealistic dedication to ideals, but in metaphysics it is the view that underlying everything is *idea* or mind or spirit or experience. The idealist affirms psychical functions as characteristic of even the most primitive units of all existence. Idealists deny that space, or extension, is a basic reality, but many idealists assert the reality of time. In process thought, discussed in chapter 6, *time* is considered real and is defined as the transition from one experience to the next. Hartshorne defines the phenomenon known as *space* as the coexistence of many lines of experiential development going on in time.

Dualism. Some metaphysicians (called dualists, a particular form of qualitative pluralism) have claimed that matter and mind are equally real, with neither explainable in terms of the

TABLE 1

VARIETIES OF METAPHYSICS

Name	Type (how many kinds of reality there are)	Quantity of Reality (how many units of reality there are)	Quality of Rea (what anything be like to be at the specific nat of reality)
Materialism (naturalism)	monistic	pluralistic	matter (ener
Dualism	pluralistic	pluralistic	mind (thought) matter (extens
Extreme pantheistic idealism (absolutism, perennialism) (Hinduism)	monistic	monistic	one Mind (plur and personality pure illusion)
Moderate pantheistic idealism (traditional Substance New Thought)	monistic	monistic	one Mind (plur and personality largely unexpla
Panentheistic idealism (psychicalism, panpsychism) (Process New Thought)	monistic	pluralistic	many minds ins one supreme M (or one Mind w many freely choosing parts)
Theistic idealism (Personalism)	monistic	pluralistic	many minds ou one supreme M
Atheistic idealism (rare)	monistic	pluralistic	many equal mi
Neutral monism (rare)	monistic	pluralistic	neutral entities organized in or way produce m in another way matter

other. In other words, dualists, unlike everybody else, believe in two kinds of reality. Most thinkers agree that dualism is untenable because there is no reasonable way to explain how mind or thought, which does not occupy space, could ever meet matter, which is extended in space. This *absolute* dualism differs from a *relative* dualism that considers mind and body to be of the same type of reality but separable at the time of death.

The terms *mind* and *matter* can be confusing, especially when an idealist denies the existence of matter. We should distinguish between matter as real in itself and matter as real in the form of a phenomenon or experience or idea. Some try to deny the reality of matter in both senses, seeing everything as illusion. New Thought denies that matter is real in itself, but affirms it as real as a form of experience. It's mind and it matters, but it's not matter, and we hope you don't mind.

Substance and Process. Whether idealist or materialist, you need to decide whether the universe is static or dynamic. This translates into believing in a *substance* or a *process* view of reality. In metaphysics, *substance* means whatever stands under (*sub stare*) phenomena; substance is whatever is basic, not dependent on anything else, but is that on which everything else depends. *Substance* can apply to material and nonmaterial reality, if both are genuinely basic. Although the word *substance* itself is neutral about the nature of the reality to which it applies, in practice the term has come to be associated with belief in continuing stuff, whether material or nonmaterial. Such stuff supposedly goes through various changes, acting and being acted on, while retaining its own existence. This admittedly gives rise to some wonderful New Thought metaphors about molding substance to fit one's heart's desire.

In contrast, *process* refers to basic reality that is itself event, change, experience. It should not be confused with the common meaning of *process* as the way in which some operation is done, as distinguished from the outcome of the procedure. Process thinkers, in the metaphysical sense, say that what appears to be enduring stuff is actually built up of momentarily existing experiences. The great metaphysical problem for New Thought,

New Age, and the rest of civilization is whether basic reality is enduring substance or process. Is the universe more like celestial Play-Doh or a giant animated sign flashing on and off? Chapter 6 should be helpful in relation to this. While civilization is pondering this weighty question, we shall take off in our time machine.

A Brief Gallop Through History

If we were to consider all the relevant philosophical background of New Thought, we'd have to go back to the earliest days of philosophy. However, we are going to skip the ancient and medieval periods, except to mention that the ancient Stoics had much of the essence of a New Thought approach. They taught that people give their worlds the colors of their own thoughts, and that (as Epictetus put it) every situation has two handles, one by which it can be borne and one by which it cannot. But the Stoics taught imperturbable resignation to one's lot, not transformation of it. They believed in a God that was all, but scarcely was love.

In a temporal hop from the ancient world of the Stoics, we'll skip over the whole Middle Ages (a thousand years without a bath, as some unappreciative wag has quipped) and land well into the modern period on the shores of seventeenth-century New England.

We all have heard of Puritanism, and we probably associate it with stern, sober people with their attention firmly fixed on a spiritual world superior to the one that we are aware of. However, Puritanism was not so otherworldly as we sometimes suppose. It appreciated scientific study of the universe, which was considered to be God's handiwork. Puritanism contained the seeds of later American practicality, best known in pragmatism, which is famous—if somewhat misunderstood—for its maxim that "if it works, it's true."

After the time of Puritan dominance came the period of the Enlightenment, coinciding with the gaining of American independence. The Enlightenment thinkers were this-worldly and optimistic, believing in the theology of deism, which maintained that God was an aloof sort of cosmic watchmaker who had made the world and wound it up so well that he had no need to bother with it later. There was no point in appealing to him for anything, and since everybody was so enlightened and reasonable, there was no need to bother much with God other than to appreciate his creation.

Historical periods tend to stand ideologically back to back, yet the seeds of a following period are sown in the one preceding it. Calvinism emphasized original sin and resulting human depravity, with one's only hope being in divine salvation—for those elected by God. In contrast, the Enlightenment of the eighteenth century emphasized reason, nature, human perfectibility, and progress: understanding the world and improving it. Typically, Americans in the nineteenth century then reacted against the Enlightenment, partly out of fear that the Enlightenment-inspired fruits of the French Revolution might threaten the gains achieved through the American Revolution.

In the first half of the nineteenth century, Romanticism—emphasizing feeling above reason—reached the United States. At the same time came a wide variety of utopian efforts to perfect people and society, with much sympathy for the downtrodden. Among the causes championed were the abolition of slavery, the prohibition of alcohol and tobacco, the institution of socialism, and the founding of communities such as Brook Farm, Fruitlands, and the Shaker communities. Exaggerated passion was in; restraint and understatement were out. It was fashionable to die young of wasting illness or unrequited love.

The quintessential American expression of philosophical Romanticism was Transcendentalism, with its most famous representative Ralph Waldo Emerson (1803–1882). The essence of Transcendentalism was reliance on intuition, which its adherents believed could transcend—go beyond—physical senses, reason, and Scripture. Drawing partly on newly translated Eastern religious writings, Transcendentalism found its way to a pantheistic outlook, holding that God is all. This contrasted sharply with the traditional Western separation of God and the world, especially with the deistic idea of an absentee God. Philosophers classify Transcendentalism as idealistic.

Transcendentalism marked only the beginning of Eastern influence in America. Two important events in the flow of Eastern thought to the West were the founding of the Theosophical Society in New York in 1875 and the World's Parliament of Religions, held in conjunction with the Columbian Exposition in Chicago in 1893. The floodgates were open thereafter for Eastern thought to permeate American civilization.

But we should not think that the nineteenth century provided smooth sailing for idealistic philosophy and religion, whether traditional supernaturalism or Transcendentalist pantheism. At the end of the two greatest decades of Transcendentalism came the naturalistic broadside fired by Charles Darwin's *The Origin of Species* in 1859. From then until now there has been a war, with fluctuating ferocity, fought over the merits of divine creation versus natural processes of evolution.

One example of materialism on the hoof was something known as the philosophy of *electrical psychology*. It appeared in the context of mesmerist thought, which is where Quimby enters the picture, as we are about to see. John Bovee Dods (1795–1872), developer of this philosophy, considered electricity to be the mediating material substance between mind and matter. He also saw electricity as the body of God. He could not conceive of anything, including mind, that did not occupy space, which means that he was a materialist. His outlook is similar to that of today's materialists who seek to explain everything in terms of different rates of vibration of something—however tenuous it may be—occupying space. Nice try, John.

Materialism, in both philosophical and popular senses, gained strength through the second half of the nineteenth century, but idealism, also in both senses, continued to flower. Then in the twentieth century, metaphysical idealism declined for decades. New Thought was one of the outlooks in which idealism survived in both centuries.

Where It All Began: Phineas Parkhurst Quimby

Where should we turn to discover the origins of New Thought? A few say to Chicago in the 1880s, but those people are emphasizing the organizational aspect of the movement. Most who have looked seriously into New Thought have seen the need to trace it back to the beginnings without which there would have been no New Thought in Chicago or anywhere else. So we turn east, not to the Orient, but to the little town of Belfast, Maine, half a century earlier. There we find a short, handsome, brilliant, self-educated clockmaker-inventor-daguerreotyper named Phineas Parkhurst ("Park") Quimby.

Quimby was born on February 16, 1802, in Lebanon, New Hampshire, but—except when away practicing healing—lived almost all his life in Belfast, where he died on January 16, 1866. He was one of seven children of a blacksmith and his wife. Reportedly, Quimby had only six weeks of schooling. He was apprenticed to a clockmaker and became a master of his trade. In addition, he invented and patented a band saw, a lock, and a steering gear for ships; and he was one of the early makers of daguerreotype photographs. He married Susannah B. Harden, and they had three sons and one daughter. He also changed civilization; how extensively we do not yet know, for his influence continues to grow. He did this by healing many people and sharing his theories with them. A few of them spread his teachings and their adaptations of them around the world in a process that continues vigorously today—just what this;book is doing.

Two mesmerizers—hypnotizers, we'd call them today—came to Belfast and gave exhibitions of their skills in the late 1830s. Quimby attended and was skeptical, especially of the first visitor, but after the second one came, Quimby decided to investigate mesmerism, or animal magnetism, himself. He discovered that he mesmerized extremely well.

Since the days of ancient Greece, thinkers have speculated on the connection of magnetism and life. They came to believe that there was a subtle magnetic fluid linking all people with one another and with the heavenly bodies. Franz (Friedrich) Anton Mesmer (1734–1815) accepted such views and brought about healings by putting people into a trance known as mesmeric sleep. He attributed the results to imparting what he supposed to be a magnetic fluid to his patients. Mesmerism became fashionable and secured the attention of two French scientific committees, one of them including U.S. ambassador Benjamin Franklin. The official conclusion attributed the results of mesmerism to "imagination," as if the use of imagination were not important.

The curative value of mesmerism was less interesting to many than were the so-called higher phenomena of mesmerism: various parapsychological happenings brought about in some mesmerized subjects. These phenomena reportedly included mind reading, sharing in the sensations of other people, seeing distant places or seeing through opaque materials wherever located, diagnosing illnesses and prescribing remedies for people, and even contacting the dead. Well, with no television, what else was there to do for entertainment?

In order to understand Quimby's interest in mesmerism, we must note that this was the Age of Heroic Medicine, of leeches and lancing, of calomel and belladonna, of doctors who probably killed more than they cured. In desperation, people would turn anywhere in search of help. After he became involved in healing, Quimby remarked that people "send for me and the undertaker at the same time; and the one who gets there first gets the case." Then too, this was an age extraordinarily interested in this relatively new and fascinating thing called science.

Quimby probably was more than ordinarily interested in the possibilities of mesmerism for healing because of an earlier incident. While still a young man, he was diagnosed as very ill with consumption (tuberculosis), and he expected to die of it. He knew of someone who had been healed by riding horseback, so Quimby—too weak to ride on a horse—decided to ride in a carriage. While doing so, he became excited and drove the horse as fast as he could. Remarkably, he felt as strong as ever when he reached the stable.

Quimby discovered that he could bring about some strange phenomena through mesmerizing a young man, Lucius Burkmar, who was particularly gifted at going into the mesmeric state. For a few years Quimby and Lucius toured New England and nearby Canada, giving demonstrations of mesmerism. Not only was Lucius diagnosing illness and prescribing simple remedies, but Quimby was mesmerically healing. As Lucius put it in his journal:

> Quimby has been doing miracles. He has cured a man that couldn't walk nor speak. It has produced a great excitement here among the people. He has been confined to his house about a year and never has spoke or walked. In one hour he made him walk about the room and speak so as to be heard in another room.

During this early exploratory time in the 1840s, Quimby made his first great discovery: there is no magnetic fluid; rather, *mind acts directly on mind.* Later he learned an even more important truth: *the explanation—the truth—is the cure.*

An important step toward Quimby's final understanding of the nature of healing came from Lucius's spontaneous mesmeric description of Quimby, who suffered back pains. Lucius described Quimby's kidneys as disintegrating, but he put his hands on Quimby's body and announced that he had put them back together. After this, Quimby had no more pain; two days later, Lucius pronounced Quimby's kidneys as good as ever. Instead of believing that Lucius had healed him, Quimby decided that Lucius had read Quimby's beliefs about his condition, and that Lucius's "ideas were so absurd that the disease vanished by the absurdity of the cure." Quimby briefly continued to use Lucius in relation to his own health, and in every instance concluded, "my troubles were of my own make."

We cannot know just what ideas influenced Quimby. Some of the possible sources were Swedenborg, Emerson, and mesmeric seer Andrew Jackson Davis, but Quimby gives no indication that their views were important to him. However, in his early "lecture notes" he does draw on Thomas Upham, a representative of the then-prevalent philosophy of Common Sense Realism, which was a reaction to the skepticism of Hume. This is important because it suggests that Quimby, ever the practical Yankee, was not given to flights of otherworldly speculation but worked out his philosophy mostly as the result of his own experiences.

Quimby developed his own clairvoyant diagnostic ability, gave up the use of Lucius, and worked out his own mode of healing. He believed that he had rediscovered the method used by Jesus. In progressing to this so-called silent method, Quimby moved from merely psychological healing (involving the influence of one human being on another) to spiritual healing (by God). Quimby hoped to publish his writings, but he was so busy with patients that he did not accomplish this. He served perhaps twelve thousand patients in Portland, Maine, from 1859 to 1865. Quimby lent some of his writings to patients, and from the 1880s onward portions of his writings appeared in print, but it was not until 1988 that the full texts were published.

Quimby's thought went through three stages of development: (1) learning that in a mesmeric state one can see through matter and at great distances; (2) "condensing" thought into mental objects for mesmeric subjects; and (3) healing with awareness of divine Wisdom working in the fertile ground of "spiritual matter." Horatio W. Dresser (1866–1954), prime interpreter of Quimby and son of two Quimby patients, emphasized the importance of Quimby's final view that what is most needed is not the natural man's molding with mind, but "the profoundest self-understanding" of one's true self as spiritual, rather than mental. Dresser summarized Quimby's outlook as follows:

1. The omnipresent Wisdom, the warm, loving, tender Father of us all . . .

2. The real man, whose life is [everlasting] in the invisible kingdom of God, whose senses are spiritual and function independently of matter.

3. The visible world, which . . . Quimby once characterized as "the shadow of Wisdom's amusements"; nature . . . [as] the outward projection or manifestation of an inward activity far more real and enduring.

4. Spiritual matter, or fine interpenetrating substance, directly responsive to thought and subconsciously embodying in the flesh the fears, beliefs, hopes, errors, and joys of the mind.

5. Disease is due to false reasoning in regard to sensations, which man unwittingly develops by impressing wrong thoughts and mental pictures upon the subconscious spiritual matter.

6. As disease is due to false reasoning, so health is due to knowledge of the truth. To remove disease permanently, it is necessary to know the cause, the error which led to it. "The explanation is the cure."

7. To know the truth about life is therefore the sovereign remedy for all ills.

In attempting to express his understanding of reality and how it works in healing, Quimby used original terminology, and his writing was confusing to many who attempted to understand it. Former patients developed Quimby's insights in varying ways, and they and their followers eventually produced what since the 1890s has been known as New Thought.

Quimby believed that creation takes place directly through sowing the seed of thought in "spiritual matter." His understanding of the creative process holds that we choose between divine Wisdom and the misconceptions of humankind, and directly receive the product of the choice. This conception foreshadows some of the essentials of Process New Thought.

As Quimby completed his earthly career, he remarked about his impending transition from earthly life to afterlife, "I do not dread the change any more than if I were going on a trip to Philadelphia." He scarcely could have known that the most important ideas to round out his system of thought would come from a five-year-old boy playing in England at the time. We do not know whether the man whom that boy became, Alfred North Whitehead, ever did learn of Quimby, but now their ideas have been united.

Spreading the Word: Warren Felt Evans

The first person to write books for what would become New Thought was former Quimby patient and Methodist-minister-turned-Swedenborgian-lay-leader Warren Felt Evans (1817–1889). The first of these books was *The Mental Cure,* published in 1869. Swedenborg's teaching that there is spiritual reality corresponding to material reality predisposed Evans toward Quimby's views. Evans practiced spiritual healing in Boston and in Salisbury, Massachusetts, but started no organization, so he has become relatively unknown. Evans contributed some Swedenborgian emphases to New Thought and added the outlooks of well-known philosophical idealists, including Berkeley and Hegel. He titled one of his chapters "The Creative Power of Thought, or Hegel's Philosophy as a Medicine." Evans summarized:

> Matter exists as a mode of consciousness in us, and is as real as that mode of thought. So disease exists as a wrong way of thinking, and to change that way of thinking for the belief of the truth, is to cure the disease, of whatever nature it is.

By 1884 Evans was quoting Emerson and identifying Emerson's Over-Soul with "the Atman of the Vedanta . . . the Christ of Paul, [and] the Adam Kadmon of the Kabala." From that time onward, Emerson became a basic source of inspiration for New Thought, which was then referred to by such names as *mind cure* and *mental science*. Evans defended the personality of God:

> In order to [have] a successful practice of the mental-cure system, it is not necessary to deny the personality of God as some have done, and reduce him to an inconceivable sea of being, an ocean of spirit without bottom or shore. . . . Such a God would be to us no God. Personality consists in Love and Wisdom, as there is no abstract impersonal love or understanding.

The writings of Evans were read widely in the United States and abroad. Charles Fillmore, cofounder of Unity, considered Evans's works to be "the most complete of all metaphysical compilations."

Diverting the Stream: Mary Baker Eddy

Mary Baker Eddy (1821–1910) was one of the people healed by Quimby. At first, she sang his praises and sought to spread his teachings. Later, she developed her Christian Science and claimed originality in discovering it, repudiating any indebtedness to Quimby. In 1875 she published her textbook, *Science and Health*.

The Christian Science church is tightly controlled from its headquarters, and has authorized literature containing its doctrines, which remain as Eddy left them. In contrast, New Thought is decidedly decentralized, and New Thoughters are free to read and to believe whatever they like. While Christian Science discourages the use of physicians, New Thought has no such restrictions, although its ideal is healing without need of medical help. The chief intellectual difference between the two is that Christian Science maintains that because God is all, matter is nothing, whereas New Thought reasons that because God is all, matter is part of God; matter is not real in itself but is real as phenomena or ideas experienced by ourselves and by God, of whom we are parts. Christian Science in its metaphysics is similar to world-denying Hinduism, while most of New Thought has a Western idealistic metaphysics.

The Movement Forms: Emma Curtis Hopkins

Emma Curtis Hopkins (1853–1925) was known as the "teacher of teachers" of New Thought. Without her work, New Thought probably would not have spread, although Quimby's supporters started organizations in Boston after Mary Baker Eddy founded her church; some of these might have developed into New Thought. At first associated with Eddy, Hopkins subsequently departed and taught independently for many years, mostly in Chicago. Among her students, who may have numbered fifty thousand, were the founders of most of the major New Thought groups. Her chief doctrinal contribution was in countering Eddy's assertion that "there is no life, substance, or intelligence in matter." Hopkins responded:

> Spirit is pure Intelligence. There is no place where matter seems to be intelligent, is there? Yet, "there is no absence of life, substance, or intelligence." If the meta-

physicians had said this, rather than "there is no life, substance, or intelligence in matter," they would have demonstrated life better than they have. For if life is Spirit, never absent, why speak of "no life"? And if Spirit is substance omnipotent, why speak of substance as "no substance" anywhere, and the same of intelligence?

Here is the essentially positive sort of metaphysical statement that would become the hallmark of New Thought.

Hopkins took the office of bishop and proceeded to ordain ministers, some of whom founded groups still important in New Thought and noted in the following sections. We shall make no attempt to deal with the separate organizations that exist within most of the major branches of New Thought, since their similarities are far more important than their differences. One thing they all have in common is women's role in leadership positions. From the start, New Thought has had many women leaders. It also has numerous African Americans, and at present some of the most prominent New Thought ministers are in either category or both.

Divine Science

The earliest New Thought denomination to emerge was Divine Science, a combination of the initial efforts of Malinda Cramer (1844–1906) and the three Brooks sisters: Nona Brooks (1861–1945), Fannie James (1854–1914), and Alethea Small (1848–1906). The sisters worked in Denver; Cramer, in San Francisco. The background of Divine Science includes both Emma Curtis Hopkins's thought and Quaker influences. Its most famous minister was Emmet Fox, who preached to large audiences in New York in the thirties and forties.

The chief Divine Science emphasis is on the omnipresence of God, or simply Omnipresence. Everything else follows from this. Divine Science proclaims to those who follow a commonsensical belief: "We have the same idea of substance; you call it matter; we call it Spirit."

Unity

Hard on the heels of Divine Science came the largest single New Thought denomination in Western culture: Unity—formally the Unity School of Christianity. It was founded in Kansas City, Missouri, by a married couple, Charles (1854–1948) and Myrtle (1845–1931) Fillmore. The Fillmores had studied with Emma Curtis Hopkins after Myrtle was healed of hereditary tuberculosis, as we have already seen—a result of a change in her belief, inspired by a lecture by a representative of Hopkins, Eugene B. Weeks. Charles Fillmore read widely in Eastern and occult writings, but he opted for the strongest emphasis on Christianity to be found in New Thought. His statement still appears monthly in *Unity* magazine:

> Unity is a link in the great educational movement inaugurated by Jesus Christ; our objective is to discern the truth in Christianity and prove it. The truth that we teach is not new, neither do we claim special revelations or discovery of new religious principles. Our purpose is to help and teach mankind to use and prove the eternal Truth taught by the Master.

Like the rest of New Thought, Unity requires no doctrinal conformity. Unity President Connie Fillmore summarizes Unity's belief system:

1. God is absolute good, everywhere present.
2. Human beings have a spark of divinity within them, the Christ spirit within. Their very essence is of God, and therefore they are inherently good also.
3. Human beings create their experiences by the activity of their thinking. Everything in the manifest realm has its beginning in thought.
4. Prayer is creative thinking that heightens the connection

with God-Mind and therefore brings forth wisdom, healing, prosperity, and everything good.

5. Knowing and understanding the laws of life, also called Truth, are not enough. A person must also live the Truth that he or she knows.

A recent Unity pamphlet adds:

> Unity is more a teaching than a creed and more an attitude than a teaching. Unity is an open-ended religion. Unity does not feel that its teachings incorporate all Truth or final Truth; the search for Truth is as much a part of Truth as finding it. Unity's teachings are more a set of directions than they are a doctrine. They are not fence posts that shut you in or shut you out; they are signposts that show you the way to Truth that you must ultimately find in yourself and for yourself.

Presumably, all branches of New Thought would apply these words to their own teachings and heartily cry, Amen!

Perhaps the best known Unity publication is *Daily Word*, a monthly collection of daily meditations as well as brief articles. The monthly magazine, *Unity*, publishes longer articles. Probably most readers of these, and many other New Thought writings, know nothing of the larger category, New Thought. Unity was a member of the International New Thought Alliance in its early days but left because the INTA did not sufficiently satisfy Charles Fillmore's understanding of what it meant to be Christian. Although the Unity School of Christianity is not a member of the INTA, the Association of Unity Churches is a member, as are many Unity churches, ministers, and laypeople.

Religious Science/Science of Mind

One of the last people to study with Emma Curtis Hopkins was Ernest Holmes (1887–1960). Holmes established Religious Science, known also as Science of Mind, the title of both the textbook that he wrote and the monthly magazine that he founded. Possibly because of his association with Hopkins, Holmes placed much emphasis on mysticism, but in New Thought a mystical approach is so common that there is little point in trying to trace its origins in any single branch. Although Religious Science agrees with the rest of New Thought in all essentials, Religious Science has the most systematic presentation of New Thought. This is partly because Holmes drew to a considerable extent on the writings of Thomas Troward (1847–1916), who was one of the most systematic and influential thinkers in the movement.

The essence of Religious Science belief is found in the "What I Believe" statement published by Ernest Holmes in the first issue of *Science of Mind* magazine in October 1927. Currently it is published as "What We Believe." Here it is presented in somewhat condensed form, with very slight rewording to accommodate the abbreviation. It affirms belief in:

God, the Living Spirit Almighty; one, indestructible, absolute, and self-existent Cause; manifesting itself in and through all creation but not absorbed by its creation.

The manifest universe as the body of God; it is the logical and necessary outcome of the infinite self-knowingness of God.

Incarnation of the Spirit in man, with all men incarnations of the One Spirit.

The eternality, the immortality, and the continuity of the individual soul, forever and ever expanding.

The Kingdom of Heaven within man and experienced to the degree that we become conscious of it.

The ultimate goal of life as a complete emancipation from all discord of every nature, and this goal as sure to be attained by all.

The unity of all life, and that the highest God and the innermost God is one God.

God as personal to all who feel this Indwelling Presence.

The direct revelation of Truth through the intuitive

and spiritual nature of man; any man may become a revealer of Truth who lives in close contact with the Indwelling God.

The Universal Spirit, which is God, operates through a Universal Mind, which is the Law of God; we are surrounded by this Creative Mind which receives the direct impress of our thought and acts upon it.

The healing of the sick through the power of this Mind.

The control of conditions through the power of this Mind.

The eternal Goodness, the eternal Loving-kindness, and the eternal Givingness of Life to all.

Our own soul, our own spirit, and our own destiny; for we understand that the life of man is God.

The most practically important part of Science of Mind is the method called Spiritual Mind Treatment. This is not basically different from the praying practices of other forms of New Thought, but it is put forth in a methodical way, with clearly distinguished steps:

1. Recognition of God's existence.
2. Unification of yourself with God (a meditative practice ideally producing something at least approaching mystical experience).
3. Realization (making real, calling into actuality what you desire, accepting, affirming, choosing your good, truth telling, firmly and confidently "speaking your word," always in the present tense, as if already accomplished).
4. Thanksgiving (gratitude).
5. Release (letting go, allowing God to work without your supervision, not pulling up the seeds that you have just planted to see whether they have sprouted yet).

In the January 1994 *Science of Mind,* Craig Carter says:

There are many ways to give a metaphysical treatment for healing, but there is only one purpose behind any treatment, which is to change the consciousness of the person giving the treatment. Generally speaking, this is done either by "argument" or by "realization," but the effect is the same.

We usually give a treatment by stating, in various ways, the Truth involved, until we finally realize that this Truth is now established, and we can "let go and let God," knowing the work is done.

Some students prefer just to see and feel and know God's perfect Presence at, in, and as the person, place or thing treated. This kind of work is a silent "realization," rather than a use of statements or words.

But whatever the method of treatment, what happens is that our own consciousness is changed: where we saw a problem, we now see Truth established. . . .

Seicho-No-Ie

An unusual offshoot of Religious Science is the Seicho-No-Ie (variously translated "house of growth" and "home of infinite life, wisdom, and abundance") Truth of Life movement. Although little known in the United States, it is influential in Japan, where it has its world headquarters. Its United States headquarters is in Gardena, California. It is probably the largest single New Thought denomination. Seicho-No-Ie sometimes is called "a ministry through publications" because of the great quantity of literature that it distributes. It is a member of the International New Thought Alliance.

Seicho-No-Ie was founded by Masaharu Taniguchi (1893–1985). In 1928 he discovered a book, *The Law of Mind in Action*, by Congregational minister Fenwick Holmes, who was associated with his brother, Ernest, in the early days of Religious Science. This book helped Taniguchi to organize his thought and to found Seicho-No-Ie in 1930, when he began publishing a magazine of that name. Seicho-No-Ie teaches standard New Thought, in addition to a distinctive form of meditation called *shinsokan* (meditation to visualize God) and certain chants. Seicho-No-Ie claims three million followers in Japan. Taniguchi also translated into Japanese the Religious Science textbook *The Science of Mind.*

Something of the spirit of Seicho-No-Ie is given in its pamphlet "You Are a Child of God!":

> The Truth of Life philosophy embraces all religions, races, and creeds. It incorporates the teachings of Christianity, Buddhism, and Shintoism and emphasizes the truth that all major religions emanate from one universal God. . . .
>
> It is dedicated to spreading the truth that man is a child of God; therefore, in reality man is divine in nature and the possessor of all of the creative powers of God. . . . We are in reality without sin, disease, poverty, pain, or suffering. . . .
>
> We believe that we can live God-like, profound lives now, and achieve a heavenly existence while still living in this world. We need only awaken to that which we already possess.

Other New Thought Groups

Originally New Thought groups were not churches, and it was only with reluctance that some of their leaders acceded to the desires of their followers to be organized as churches. Boston's Metaphysical Club is an example of a New Thought organization that lasted about seven decades and never became a church. There are still some nonchurch New Thought centers. Strong sentiment against the church model, at least for the International New Thought Alliance, was shown in 1993, when the membership meeting of the INTA rejected a proposal to gain significant tax advantages by technically constituting the organization as a church. Despite that financial temptation, the proposal was defeated. The Homes of Truth is the name of an early association of New Thought centers; one of the Homes survives. A small group of New Thought churches is the Church of Truth (until several years ago Church of the Truth). There are numerous independent New Thought churches, some of them incorporating Science of Mind into their names without belonging to any formally organized branch of Religious Science.

Bringing It Together:
The International New Thought Alliance

The umbrella organization that links all the New Thought denominations along with independent organizations and individuals is the International New Thought Alliance. It was the outgrowth of various New Thought conventions beginning around the turn of the century, receiving its present name in 1914. As the name indicates, it is an alliance, a coming together of different New Thought organizations and individuals, for the purpose of sharing ideas and inspiration and facilitating activities of its members. In addition to presenting the "Declaration of Principles," quoted in full in chapter 1, the current INTA general information brochure contains numerous amplifying statements, including the following:

> The International New Thought Alliance is a free and open alliance of truth-motivated individuals and organizations who desire to unfold and practice a positive lifestyle of spiritual maturity. INTA unites individuals and organizations with common determination to bring out the best in all through an understanding of these eternal verities. . . .
> INTA is a year-round working organization, democratic in structure, and serves as the means through which metaphysical schools, churches, and centers of like mind can work together.

The INTA has more than a hundred districts around the planet, reflecting its significant international growth, especially in recent years. It publishes a quarterly magazine, *New Thought*. In addition to the annual INTA Expo, many of its districts put on their own meetings, with varying frequency. The INTA looks both to the past and to the future. It recently established its archives, with a professional archivist, at its headquarters in Mesa, Arizona. As stated in the brochure:

> New Thought is a synonym for growth, development and perpetual progress. It does not deal with limitations. It sets no bounds to the soul's progress and sees limitless transcendental faculties within each soul.
>
> New Thought may be said to possess a fixed ideal; that of an eternal search for Truth.

Having glimpsed the philosophical and historical background of New Thought, we are now ready to tackle its religious background. This will include tiptoeing past the occult and strolling through the divine kennel before gazing at mysticism and grappling with evil. So grab your walking stick and your derby hat and come along.

3

*

Religious Background of New Thought

*A*fter our expedition into the complexities of metaphysics, we may turn to the topic of religion with the happy assumption that it will be vastly simpler. Alas, we shall be wrong if we hold to that hope. Religion is about as complicated as is metaphysics. However, we are going to omit most of that complexity, so this chapter should be less challenging than the previous.

Religion and Spirituality

There are many conflicting definitions of religion. Some emphasize the solitariness of religious experience, some the community aspect of religion. Some stress belief, some feeling and attitude, some action (both ceremonial and in the world doing good works). Philosopher Edgar S. Brightman maintained that the most comprehensive definition of religion must include belief, attitude, and action in relation to what one considers the ultimate source and promoter of value.

We might consider *spirituality* the raw material out of which the various religions are manufactured. The term is used in various ways. In recent years it has referred to the inner, value-centered life of people in their relation to the divine apart from organized religion, or at least not dependent upon it.

We are seeing the ascendancy of spirituality over religion in the minds of many, ranging from mystics and their kindred near-death experiencers to people who have had no unusual experience yet hunger for something beyond the standard forms of religiosity. It is therefore important to seek approaches to religion that take away something of its relatively bad name. At its best, religion can be spirituality, or at least a major repository of spirituality. At its worst, religion may restrict spirituality and hide or obscure it within buildings, rituals, and allegiance to man-made authorities and doctrines.

The Spiritual-Mystical and the Occult

Not all experiences that go beyond the range we consider usual (normal) are of a religious or spiritual nature. It may be that no experience is religious, or nonreligious, apart from our interpretation of it. Any experience can be interpreted in various ways. Perhaps the most commonly disputed type of experience is that called *mystical*. A mystic is one who experiences what he or she considers unity with God. For the mystic this is the ultimate perspective, the most utterly sane insight; for some psychiatrists it indicates mental instability. Mystical enlightenment may come as the result of long meditation, or it may dawn as a complete surprise. In any case, it leaves its recipient profoundly changed.

The mystic typically goes through stages variously counted and named by different observers: (a) a preparatory stage, sometimes divided into conversion and purgation, (b) an illuminative stage in which he or she literally sees the light, and (c) a fully unitive stage of oneness with God. Sometimes between the second and third stages there may be a loss of a sense of the divine (the loss called the "dark night of the soul"), and some Eastern mystics speak of a final stage of dissolution of human selfhood. The progression onward in mysticism is called the *mystic way*.

The essence of mysticism is love. William James gives the characteristics of mystical experience as (a) ineffability, (b) knowledge-giving quality, (c) brevity, and (d) passivity. Anglican writer Evelyn Underhill emphasizes that mysticism (a) is traditionally active and practical, (b) has exclusively spiritual aims, not concerned with exploring or improving the world, (c) has

God as the personal object to be loved, rather than known about, and (d) produces a remaking of character through the releasing of a latent form of consciousness. This is a qualitative awareness, easily distinguishable from any others by anyone who has the experience. Richard M. Bucke, a nineteenth-century Canadian psychiatrist, impressively presents many cases of mystical consciousness in his classic *Cosmic Consciousness.*

The beautiful inclusiveness of mysticism is shown in a quotation from a book by Beatrice Bruteau, *Radical Optimism:*

> Nobody denies that dividing, as a vehicle for better understanding, is useful. But along comes the mystic and puts the separated things together, and all the rational people cry Paradox! or worse, Heresy! From the mystic's point of view, however, there is no paradox, nothing bewildering or mysterious.
>
> The mystic sees very clearly on the basis of experience how the unity is there. . . . Subject and object are merged in a single consciousness. One is both oneself and intimately united with all others. What one does is done by both oneself *and* the Supreme Being. You don't have to choose between them. People sometimes say: I didn't do that, God did it. But when one goes a little deeper, one finds that the action is both one's own and God's, a single act born of confluent energies.

Getting ahead of ourselves a little, we note that Bruteau shows the kinship of mysticism and the process thinking that we'll cover in chapter 6:

> The Creator is fully present in the creature, because the creature *is* God's act of creating, not some product left over after the act of creation is finished. And the act of creating *is* the active presence of the Creator.

There may be no more misused word than *mysticism.* It often is confused with magic or spookiness. Using the term correctly, many advocates of mysticism claim that mysticism is the great common denominator of all religions. However, some scholars maintain that mysticism is significantly different from one religion to another.

When you go beyond the range of usual experience, you can follow either of two paths: the mystic or the *psychic*. As we have seen, the mystic is concerned with union with God, who is Love. The psychic is concerned with the extension of knowledge and activity in realms beyond the usual senses. The area concerned with the psychic long has been called *occultism* (from *occultus*, hidden, covered). For more than a century it has been known as *psychical research* (as in the British and American Societies for Psychical Research, started in the 1880s). For more than half a century it has also been known as *parapsychology*, especially when associated with laboratory research in the area. Sometimes occultism or occult philosophy is referred to as *esotericism*, especially when considered in the context of overall spiritual orientation. The realm of the psychic includes:

Extrasensory perception (ESP)

- telepathy: mind reading
- clairvoyance: supersensory knowledge about material objects or events not obtained from another mind
- precognition: extrasensory knowing about a future event
- retrocognition: extrasensory knowing about a past event
- mental mediumship (channeling), which could be considered a form of telepathy: obtaining information from a discarnate being

Psychokinesis (PK) (the direct application of mind to matter beyond one's own muscles)

- psychokinesis proper: the direct, purposeful action of human mind on physical objects
- telekinesis: the spontaneous movement of objects without observable force or energy
- physical mediumship: the production of physical objects,

especially those having the shape of the body, or part of it, of a deceased person
- poltergeists: habitual disturbances associated with a particular place or person
- paranormal healing

Perhaps magic should be mentioned here—not magic as trickery performed for amusement, but as genuine wonder-working. Magic that purports to be genuine is divided into white magic, performed to do good, and black magic, done to do harm. Although recently there have been objections to recognizing magic as clearly different from various religious practices, magic often has been distinguished from religion on the ground that magic is an attempt to work one's own will on the powers that be, whereas religion is an attempt to bring oneself into conformity with a divine will.

Whatever may be the truth about claims made in these areas, it is important to keep them separated from mysticism. However, there are overlaps: mystics also may see visions, which are psychical rather than mystical experiences. Whether the light associated with mystical experience should be considered psychical is open to question. The great test is the presence of overwhelming love in mysticism, a life-changing reality qualitatively different from ordinary experience. In contrast, psychical experience is extension of ordinary experience beyond its usual range in the physical world or into dimensions not ordinarily experienced. Mystical experience can be thought of as a vertical extension of experience, while psychical experience is a horizontal extension.

Theologian Paul Tillich, who defined religion as "ultimate concern," considered the existence of separate religious and secular realms to be an emergency measure based on humankind's estrangement from its true being. One of the characteristics of New Thought is that it attempts to remove the wall between the sacred and the secular. It finds the spiritual not so much in the sense of some unapproachable yet fascinating *mysterium tremendum* (Rudolf Otto's term), but more in the mystic's magnificent, overpowering realization of God as overwhelming Love. New Thought appropriates this love not only as a source of inspiration in daily life, as Brother Lawrence, the author of *The Practice of the Presence of God*, did, but as a power and guide in bringing about ends usually considered secular.

There are various ways of slicing up religion. One way is to consider the standard brands such as (alphabetically) Buddhism, Christianity, Hinduism, Islam, Judaism, and others. A better procedure for our purposes takes note of the types of approach to religion found in varying degrees in probably all traditions.

Basically, there are the ways of the priest, the prophet, and the mystic. The priestly, or sacramental, path emphasizes sacred objects and formal observances. The prophetic approach stresses revelation, receiving messages believed to come directly from God; it often denounces religionists for falling away from divine ways. The primary meaning for *prophet* is *one who speaks out;* only secondarily does it relate to one who foretells the future. The mystic way is the way of personal union with the divine, which is most commonly held to be God but may sometimes take a similar sense of oneness with one's soul or with nature. A roughly similar way of classifying religious types refers to ways of rites and works; ways of knowledge; and ways of piety, devotion, or mysticism. Each religion tends to favor one of the three emphases over the others.

New Thought at its best is much inclined toward mysticism, both for its own sake and as part of the process of attaining overall wholeness. This combination is suggested in the name of one of the smaller New Thought groups, the Society of Pragmatic Mysticism. However, some New Thoughters tend to treat New Thought as if it were a matter of knowledge, to the exclusion of mysticism. The publisher's preface to Ella Wheeler Wilcox's 1902 (1993 reprint) *The Heart of the New Thought* says:

> That which was vague, mystic, unreal, has become, in the hands of Mrs. Wilcox, a lovable philosophy of simplest construction. The backbone of this philosophy is The Power of Right Thought.

Many who have emphasized impressing the subconscious mind might well agree, as in Joseph Murphy's *The Power of Your*

Subconscious Mind, which recognizes God but concentrates on subconscious mind. On the other hand, great leaders of New Thought have emphasized moving forth from mystical awareness to claiming one's good. A recent book by Dorothy Elder, *From Metaphysical to Mystical,* urges New Thoughters to move more clearly to mysticism from what the book, in a popular way, refers to as metaphysics. This brings us to some other important matters of classification and terminology with regard to God.

Breeds of God

Since the day when the ancient Greek philosopher Xenophanes pointed out that people fashion gods in their own likenesses and claimed that animals would do the same if they could, people have been aware that we make our own conceptions of God. Most people believe that God makes us in his image. Now some are starting to realize that at least in a tiny way, we also help to make God what he is. Most of New Thought has not gone that far, but New Thought has realized that God has put us in charge of making ourselves what we are and what we shall be.

It makes little or no sense to ask whether one believes in God without considering what kind of God one believes in. One cannot consistently believe in all the conceptions of God that are available. So we need to consider what God is like. The Divine Kennel below (adapted from Alan's book, *A Guide to the Selection and Care of Your Personal God*) will help to show how competing notions of God are built up from basic views of God's characteristics.

Abbreviations for Attributes of God

I	Inside the universe (immanent)
O	Outside the universe (transcendent)
U	Upstairs (inactive, changeless, eternal [timeless])

D	Downstairs (active, growing, temporal)
Archaic Terrorer:	the ID God of *primitive theism* (somewhat like the Freudian id), powerful and capricious.
Yapping Heel-Nipper:	also ID (or DI, drill instructor); essentially like the Terrorer, but more ethically oriented.
Purebred High-Nosed:	the OU God, or when at least occasionally concerned with the world, the slumming High-Nosed, the God of *classical theism,* who creates the world (universe) but is unmoved by it. The Extremely High-Nosed is the God of *deism.*
World Woofer:	the IUD God of *pantheism,* one with the universe, yet unchanging, so baffles or prevents mental conception.
Mixed Breed:	IOUD God of *panentheism,* the God of cocreation through ever-growing, interactive love—as panentheist Charles Hartshorne puts it, "the unimaginable actual love of the unimaginable vastness of actual things."

One thing about God that is not covered in this chart seems clear: She has a sense of humor.

Religion in the United States

Religion is one of the most common sides of human culture, but it varies vastly from one place and time to another. Nowhere is it more fascinating and distinctive than in the United States.

Probably more than at any other time and place in history, American religion has been a freewheeling experience and interpret-it-yourself phenomenon. Consequently, religion as found in America may be more nearly pure spirituality than other religion has been.

No doubt, it is going too far to suggest that there is essentially only one American religion, but there is enough truth to the claim that there is an American religion to make the matter worth exploring. Certainly there are some characteristics that set American religion apart from religion in comparable countries.

In the first place, Americans are much more united than Europeans in believing in the existence of God and of life after death. Various polls show that well over 90 percent of Americans believe that God exists. A Gallup poll found that 77 percent believe in heaven, and 76 percent think they have a good chance of getting there.

Kosmin and Lachman, in *One Nation Under God: Religion in Contemporary American Society,* conclude that

> The vast majority of Americans consider themselves to be religious and are not afraid to admit it. For most, *religion* means a personal affirmation of faith in God and an identification with a religious denomination, but it does not necessarily mean joining or being an active member of that particular group. It is more of a private commitment than a shared experience.

Members of probably all religious groups in America are becoming more individualistic. They will ignore whatever teachings they do not like. Surveys have found that some major beliefs of American Catholics bear little relationship to the teachings of their church. The typical American bows to no one in formulation of his or her beliefs, whether in government, religion, or elsewhere. If a belief does not pass muster in the individual's inspection of it, it is rejected. Quimby was one of those who most clearly exemplified this attitude.

Regardless of whether there is a distinctive, common-denominator American religion, the United States certainly has provided fertile soil for the origination and growth of religions. New Thought was only one of the outlooks coming out of nineteenth-century America. In his *The American Religion* Harold Bloom pays special attention to some of them, including Mormonism (the Church of Jesus Christ of Latter-day Saints), Christian Science, Seventh-Day Adventism, Jehovah's Witnesses, Pentecostalism, and the Southern Baptists.

Bloom considers American religions to be experiential, individually oriented approaches to reality significantly different from other branches of their churches, in the cases of those that share ancient denominational traditions. Bloom finds American religion to be characterized by

> three fundamental principles. The first is that what is best and oldest in us goes back well before the Creation. The second is that what makes us free is knowledge, a history of facts and events, rather than a belief founded upon mere assent. The third is that this freedom has a solitary element in it, an element imbued by the loneliness of belated American time, and American experience of the abyss of space. What holds these principles together is the American persuasion, however muted or obscured, that we are mortal gods, destined to find ourselves again in worlds as yet undiscovered.

Now that we have seen something of what spirituality and religion can be, especially in their American permutations, it is appropriate to turn to the essentially Christian background of New Thought.

New Thought as Reformation

A religious reformation is intended to be just that: a reform, a correction, a return to something that people feel has been lost or distorted. If it goes off in an entirely new direction, it is either something entirely new or it is a deformation rather than a reformation.

There have been numerous arguments as to what constitutes a Christian reformation. To determine this, we must first understand what Christianity was in the first place.

The Jesus of the Gospels is quite a different person from the Christ of the Epistles. For better or for worse, St. Paul came along after Jesus' death, resurrection, and ascension. It was St. Paul and the apostles who developed the early Christology, and it may well be that without it, Christianity would never have blossomed into the movement that was able to spread to the boundaries of the known world. Then came the fall of Rome and the Dark Ages, and Christianity was affected along with the rest of Western culture. The Renaissance, the Reformation led by Martin Luther, and the Enlightenment, with the rise of science, all also had bearing on Christianity as a part of Western culture. By the mid-nineteenth century, entering a Christian church of any denomination was a very different experience from walking beside an itinerant Jewish rabbi along the shores of the first-century Sea of Galilee.

We might well think of what Jesus taught and did as *primitive Christianity.* Many would agree that that primitive Christianity has been lost, drowned in a tidal wave of atrocities perpetrated in the name of religion, or worse, in the name of Christianity. In any case, many people do not find the strength and comfort they seek in what the Christian church has become.

Just Do What the Man Said

What might a return to primitive Christianity entail? First, it would involve a careful reading of the best translations available of what we believe to be the words and deeds of Jesus. Many Christian denominations today put little or no emphasis on the reading of the Bible, let alone on attempts to interpret it meaningfully.

Second, without getting caught up in quibbles about Christology, or whose heresy is in or out of vogue this week, or whose followers bribed the Imperial Guard with Numidian stallions in order to get whose beliefs enshrined as orthodox, it would involve a sincere effort to live by the teachings of Jesus and to emulate his actions. This means loving (expressing good will to) one another, healing the sick through prayer as much as possible, and "preaching the Gospel to the poor," which presumably has to mean some sort of prosperity teaching. It means viewing God as a loving Father, and the universe as a friendly place in which one's desires can be met: "Ask, and it shall be given you; seek, and ye shall find; knock, and it shall be opened unto you" (Matt. 7:7; Luke 11:9).

Theologians well argue that Jesus must have been both human and divine, or what he did was of limited usefulness. In some way he bridged the apparent gap between human beings and their Creator. But the details of how all this comes to be are irrelevant to most of us as we strive to get through the day.

As far as we can determine, Jesus laid tremendous emphasis on the power and importance of love, first of God, then of our neighbors and ourselves. Living by this principle himself, he showed great compassion for the sick of body and mind, performing many healings that we can consider miraculous, especially if *miraculous* means involving a law of nature that we do not yet understand. He violated numerous taboos to show love for despised groups such as Samaritans, and he had only contempt for the hypocrisy of the Pharisees, who laid great importance on observing the letter of the Law at the expense of the spirit of it. He lived a prosperous existence despite owning little or nothing. He emphasized the importance of a childlike faith. His first miracle was turning water into not just wine but good wine, at a marriage feast, to keep the party going and avoid embarrassment to the host. He did not embrace asceticism in his own life, and although he went apart frequently to pray, his ministry was in the world, not in a cloister. Above all, he did not ask to be worshiped. He did say that we could pray in his name, and he instituted a feast shared in love as a perpetual recall of him.

The founders of the various New Thought denominations were all from Christian backgrounds (with the exception of the founder of Seicho-No-Ie). However, traditional Christianity had not met their needs, particularly their needs for healing. Quimby believed that he had rediscovered the lost healing techniques of Jesus. The Fillmores laid great stress on the teachings of Jesus and the Christ consciousness: "we have the mind of Christ" (1 Cor. 2:16). Without getting into arguments about dogma, New Thought sees Jesus as a role model, the wayshower, our elder brother. Yes, Jesus was unquestionably divine, made in the likeness and image of God. And so are we! This is our great hope, that we can emulate him because we are like him in kind, if not in degree. He himself told us, "Greater works than these shall [ye] do" John 14:12. Perhaps he was special and unique in other ways, but that is unimportant, so long as we are able to emulate him.

To strip away all the aggregation of beliefs and doctrines that have grown up around a simple message of love, to return to doing what the man said to do, to rise in consciousness as he did—this is a true reformation. Religion as mandatory rituals and ceremonials and man-made doctrines pales in comparison to spirituality, to the attempt to find God and our mission in the world, our purpose for being here. Spirituality is walking our own spiritual path, not one prescribed by anyone else, no matter how spiritual. We can learn from others, especially from scholars who have devoted their lives to study of the Bible or the life of Jesus, but in the last analysis, "You must walk that lonesome valley/ You have to walk it by yourself/ No, nobody else can walk it for you." Even the twelve apostles, schooled by Jesus himself, were fallible human beings. They didn't have all the answers. There is no substitute for taking responsibility for your own life, even your own spiritual life.

Believe in Jesus or Believe Jesus?

To belong to most traditional Christian churches, you must *believe in* Jesus. This means believing what you have been taught about Jesus and what he has done or can do. It may or may not involve deep emotional conviction on your part. But to *believe* Jesus means to believe what the man said and to try it out for yourself. This is what he told us to do. He said we could trust the teachings of the Old Testament Law, but he urged us to observe the spirit, not the letter of it. He said we could easily tell whose example to follow—"By their fruits ye shall know them" (Matt. 7:20)—and he used this principle himself to demonstrate that he was the promised Messiah in response to inquiries from John the Baptist: "The blind receive their sight, and the lame walk, the lepers are cleansed, and the deaf hear, the dead are raised up, and the poor have the Gospel preached to them" (Matt. 11:5).

Healing Within Traditional Churches

In the Old Testament, sickness is interpreted as the result of *sin* (from a Greek word that means "missing the mark"), and healing is the work of God, as the neighbors of the Hebrews also recognized. In the New Testament, it is obvious that healing played a large part in Jesus' ministry, and that he intended it to do so in that of his followers. He commissioned them: "Heal the sick, cleanse the lepers, raise the dead, cast out devils: freely ye have received, freely give" (Matt. 10:1; cf. Mark 6:7 and Luke 9:1–6). Healing is seen in the context of overall faith and salvation. As the church developed, healing sometimes was of central importance, sometimes peripheral.

From such accounts as we have, we know that the apostles and their successors in the early Christian church were able to do healing miracles similar to those of Jesus. Through the centuries, this knowledge and ability have faded. In the Roman Catholic church, the sacrament of unction, once used in the belief that it could heal the sick, became reserved only for the dying. In the Middle Ages, Europe was swept by terrible plagues, and miraculous healings became few and far between. A few people and places have become famous for healing; probably the most noted is the grotto in Lourdes, France. But even they are mostly sought as a last resort, not in a routine sense or with strong conviction.

The Reformation and the Enlightenment did little to help matters. As people turned away from religion and toward science to solve their problems, and science for its part sought to rid itself of old medieval superstitions, healings involving the power of mind, or even natural remedies, became scarce.

Most people from traditional Christian backgrounds believe that a miracle involves the suspension or violation of some law of nature, presumably by God himself. This would mean that

God was either inconsistent and undependable, or that he could be influenced by the pleadings of numerous or influential people. Yet St. Peter said, "God is no respecter of persons" (Acts 10:34). So Christians have tended—most of the time—not even to expect a miracle.

By the middle of the nineteenth century, heroic medicine in America was killing more people than it was helping. In the face of desperate ignorance, some people were ready and eager for change. When word came from France of a man named Mesmer with seemingly miraculous powers, despite what seems to us today flimsy evidence, an uneducated clockmaker from Maine with serious physical ailments of his own and little faith in traditional Christianity became interested. As Quimby gradually realized that the power to heal lay in his own mind in contact with divine mind, he was in fact rediscovering the healing power of Jesus. Regardless of his theology, which was by most standards a bit strange, he was in the truest sense a Christian, one who was doing his best to live the teachings of Jesus. The time had come for a restoration of spiritual healing.

This book's primary concern is with the form of spiritual healing that became known as New Thought. Another form of spiritual healing in recent times came through Christian healers with conventional views of the nature of God and of the work of the Holy Spirit in the world. This included three relatively separate developments: the European healing movement, the Holiness movement arising from Methodism, and the Pentecostal-Charismatic movements that evolved out of the Holiness movement. We'll ignore the European side of it, partly because after some years, the contributions of the European movement were taken note of by the American and incorporated into it. England and Australia made some contributions, but the central focus can well be considered American.

When nineteenth-century people started emphasizing the presence of God and the gifts of the Spirit (1 Cor. 12:4–11), healings followed. Faith healing came to be associated largely with the Holiness movement. This healing was carried over into the Pentecostal movement, which began in 1901, when speaking in tongues (glossolalia) came to the fore. When Pentecostalism moved into the mainline Protestant and Roman Catholic churches in the 1960s, that aspect of it became known as the Charismatic movement. Among the best-known names in this more than century-long line of development are Ethan O. Allen, Elizabeth Mix, Charles Parham, John Alexander Dowie, Aimee Semple McPherson, Kathryn Kuhlman, and Oral Roberts.

New Thought arose more directly out of a desire for healing than did nineteenth-century faith healing, which came as a by-product of the seeking of signs to accompany salvation.

Blending of New Thought Techniques and Revivalist Christianity

Richard Quebedeaux, in *By What Authority: The Rise of Personality Cults in American Christianity,* refers to popular religion in America as a blend of New Thought techniques and revivalistic experience of being born again.

The first half of the nineteenth century in America was a heady time of religious rebellion, along with overall democratizing of American life. As Ahlstrom puts it, in *A Religious History of the American People,* it was a time when "farmers became theologians, offbeat village youths became bishops, odd girls became prophets." There was a revival of *enthusiasm* (emotional religion). Revivalism includes perfectionism (perfect sanctification, holiness), millennialism (expecting soon the second coming of Jesus), universalism (the salvation of everyone), and illuminism (new revelations of God).

Revivalism is a term that can be used in various ways, but here it means a form of Christianity that emphasizes the necessity of personal experience of salvation, with an overall conservative interpretation of the Bible and its importance in culture. Revivalism is associated with camp meetings and similar religious gatherings. Among the names associated with it are Charles Finney, Dwight L. Moody, Billy Sunday, and Billy Graham. Revivalism is part of the larger category of evangelicalism, the most conservative part of which came to be called fundamentalism. Revivalism came to be especially identified with Holiness and Pentecostal religion.

Revivalism was filled with the doom-and-gloom (apart from salvation) side of Christianity, and was highly suspicious of any intellectualizing. But like New Thought, it was an experiential religion. New Thought incorporated into itself a rationalistic approach that sought to include scientific discoveries. Revivalism generally resisted science, especially Darwinian evolution. Revivalism needed the techniques of New Thought, and a few New Thoughters may welcome the stamp of conventional acceptance that association with pervasive popular religion gives.

Quebedeaux maintains that "upward mobility, in the context of pluralism and the principles of voluntary association, is the root cause of the growth of accommodation within popular religion as a whole—a process to make it more appealing to mass culture." Religious movements move to greater acceptance as people of higher, more prosperous classes accept them. As Pentecostal and Charismatic religion spreads and finds acceptance among religious leaders, so New Thought may find increasing acceptance alone and in combination with other religions that incorporate New Thought's insights, albeit with varying degrees of awareness and frankness about their source.

Solving the Problem of Evil

In addition to the need for healing, all religions—and philosophies—must wrestle with the problem of evil. We can all look around the world and see what we would clearly label as evil. Some would say that it is an illusion, that it isn't really there. Most find this explanation unsatisfactory. Many say, therefore, that in addition to the power of God, who is Good, there must be a second power at work in the universe: a power of evil, often personified as the devil. Traditional Christianity teaches that the devil is a fallen angel, part of God's creation that went wrong.

This makes evil a twofold problem. If God is all-good and all-powerful, how come there is evil at all? And if there is a devil, how come God's power or ability as universe designer is so limited/flawed that things came to such a pass? Some say God sends evil to punish people for misdeeds, but that is unworthy of a merciful God, and means that at least some of his creatures by being merciful are better than God—another problem. Is God a weakie, or a meanie?

New Thought, as we have seen, teaches that there is only one Presence and Power, and that power is good. And unlike Hinduism or Christian Science, it does not see evil as *maya*, illusion. If you don't believe it, kick the next flat tire you see. Evil is good that is immature or misdirected. It has no power of its own; it has only the power that our minds give to it. It doesn't have to be destroyed or fought, any more than when you come into a darkened room and turn on the light, you have to chase the darkness away. It is dealt with by thinking about and working to bring about the good that you want in its place: "Whatsoever things are true ... lovely ... of good report, if there be any virtue, and if there be any praise, think on these things" (Phil. 4:8).

No matter how terrible a situation seems to be, there is always good in it, because there is always God in it, for God is everywhere and all is in God. He is there as a source of all the love and intelligence that we need to deal with whatever we have to face and triumph over it.

According to the process philosophy described in chapter 6, any conversion of potentiality to actuality is, to that extent, good. To the extent that one fails to live up to the possibilities offered by God, one produces evil, or badness. The major point is that there is no cosmic force, no devil, acting in opposition to God's goodness, just the free choices of innumerable choosers throughout existence.

Reclaiming Mysticism and Putting It to Work

If mysticism is the direct experiencing of God, Jesus was unquestionably a mystic. There have been mystics throughout the history of the Christian church, although they are often unpopular because they are not dependent on the church for guidance but seek it independently from God as they know him. Sometimes they have even been persecuted. Occasionally the world confuses the mystic with the psychotic.

Nevertheless, in terms of spirituality, what could be more glorious than a mystical experience, or a series of them? What more could we seek than experiences of oneness with God?

The conventional revivals of interest in faith healing for the most part do not attempt to emulate the mystical relationship that Jesus had with "the Father within, [who] doeth the work." They are still mainly reserved as a last resort, when medicine fails, hoping that God will heed the pleas of the suffering and suspend some law of nature to permit healing. It is New Thought that understands that we are punished *by* our sins, not *for* them, and that by rising in consciousness we can contact the Divine Intelligence within, learn what we need to learn, and straighten out our thinking—and our lives.

If we want no more than reasonably satisfying spiritual experiences and conventional Christian understandings, we would have no reason to go beyond this approach to healing, in the broadest sense. However, if we desire spiritual depth and practical outworkings of it in our life, as well as solid theoretical foundations to explain what is going on, we have good reason to turn to New Thought, especially now, when it is beginning to rethink its foundations in terms of a process panentheism.

The existence of both New Thought and faith healing (to say nothing of Christian Science and other forms of healing emphasizing the use of divine and/or human mind) shows that there is no single exclusively effective approach to healing through nonphysical means. Anyone with faith in the effectiveness of whatever means he or she is using can tap the universal healing power and achieve amazing results. There is no substitute for simple childlike faith, such as Jesus called for. However, this faith can stand alone or can be united with various intellectual understandings and mystical experiences. This leads us to the topic of stages of faith.

Doing It in Stages

Psychiatrist Scott Peck, in his *Further Along the Road Less Traveled*, following James Fowler, who in turn is following Lawrence Kohlberg and Erik Erikson, outlines various stages of spiritual growth. These are developmental stages that all children go through, but many adults do not mature fully and remain stuck in an early stage. Peck telescopes six stages into four: Stage One, "chaotic/antisocial," "people of the lie." Stage Two is "formal/institutional," "adherence to the letter of the law," the category into which most churchgoers fall. Stage Three is "skeptic/individual," which parallels adolescence in its breaking away from traditional religion, yet it continues to seek truth. Stage Four is "mystical/communal," those who see "a cohesion beneath the surface of things," a state going beyond the letter of the law to its spirit. They differ from Stage Two primarily in being "comfortable living in a world of mystery" rather than "uncomfortable when things aren't cut-and-dried." All great religions seem somehow to be able to speak to people in both Stages Two and Four.

Jesus, speaking literally of children but by implication referring to people's stage of spiritual development, warned that for anyone who undermines the faith of a Stage Two person, "it were better for him that a millstone were hanged about his neck, and that he were drowned in the depth of the sea" (Matt. 18:6; cf. Mark 9:42 and Luke 17:2). This childlike faith can bring about miracles because of an uplifted consciousness that we would do well to emulate. New Thought provides the royal road to Stage Four, as a faith that raises human consciousness, partly by incorporating advances in science and philosophy. But we need to remember, as authority on the integration of psychology and religion Paul Vitz remarked, "What Scotty calls Stage Four is the beginning."

4

*

New Thought Expands: From Health to Wealth and Happiness

New Thought's original concern was with the healing of the body. Quimby did not teach success; however, his successors (no pun intended) soon realized that the power of the mind extended further than the health of the body alone.

In metaphysics, as we have seen, idealism says that the fundamental building blocks of the universe are mental, not material, even though this universe appears to be made of matter that is not mental experience. In Quimby's day, and for decades afterward, a mechanically oriented society could scoff at the notion of mind power, which seemed to fly in the face of common sense. We now know that despite looking and feeling solid, everything in the universe is really made up of subatomic particles whirling and dancing and shining, with lots of space between them, subject to change by being observed. But then, any elementary schoolteacher who has had the principal walk in on a class session can attest that the act of observing changes that which is being observed!

Just as our understanding of the physical universe has evolved, so have our ideas about God evolved and expanded. The first great breakthrough came when we went from believing in many gods (my god can lick your god) to one God. Then we progressed from believing that God was transcendent, off in space somewhere, to understanding that he was immanent: "closer is

He than breathing, nearer than hands and feet." Instead of being off in space, we could conceive of God as everywhere (pantheism). Most recently, we are beginning to understand that everywhere is in God (panentheism).

In chapter 2 we traced some of this developing understanding of God, from a monolith to one supreme Mind with many freely choosing parts. We can now begin to understand that if we are all part of God and we are growing, then God must be growing, changing not in perfect character, but in experience. God is not more perfect at one time than another, but God is constantly getting richer in experience. What greater foundation for self-esteem could there be than knowing that by our experiences we are enriching God? A wonderful old story concerns a statue of Jesus that had its hands blown off in time of war. Someone hung a sign around the statue's neck reading, "I have no hands but yours." It is literally true of God. We are God individualized (initiated by God and completed by ourselves) at the place where we are. We are certainly not all there is to God, but we are part of God's body. We don't need to be saved, for we were never lost. We do frequently drift away from attention to God, as a radio signal drifts, and we need to realign ourselves. That's one good definition of prayer.

The universe is basically good. What else could it be as God's body? We are exactly where we need to be in order to learn what we need to learn, and on some level, everything, even evil and suffering, makes sense in some way and fits into the divine scheme of things. God does not send suffering; we choose it, but God can bring out the good inherent in any situation. The mystic senses this oneness, this ultimate rightness and goodness. In New Thought, it is called divine order, and people like to go around decreeing it. But it is there all the time, and our prayers simply enable us to see it. This state of uplifted consciousness, this sense that everything is right and good, is what heals, because it gets the destructive thinking out of the way and permits the flow of life. There's plenty of room for improvement, and God's perfect possibilities keep rolling down the assembly line for us to choose, fresh-baked every moment.

You are the only thinker in your world, and you can therefore understand that we really do create our world with our thoughts. There does seem to be a collective human race consciousness, made up of past experiences and influencing us, but our own thinking is primary. Consequently, our own thinking determines whether we succeed or fail in attracting conditions necessary for us to thrive in all ways. This includes acquiring knowledge about money and how it works, as well as about people and how they work, or the principles of balance that lead to physical wellness and the overcoming of disease. There's a saying that when the student is ready, the teacher will appear; let us point out that the teacher may or may not be a person.

Our beliefs are our thoughts that hang around a lot, and we may acquire erroneous beliefs in numerous ways, most notably in childhood. Erroneous beliefs act as self-fulfilling prophecies. If we understand our world as a world created by our thoughts or ideas, we can also understand the interrelatedness of everything in our lives. In recent years, as medical costs have soared, more and more people have been looking into alternative or holistic medicine, which considers everything in a person's lifestyle a contribution to wellness or illness: diet; exercise; balance of work, play, and rest; doing what you love; and Consideration Number One: *attitude*. And what is your attitude but your thoughts!

I Want to Be Happy

Happiness, as analyzed by sages from Aristotle to Barry Neil Kaufman (*Son-Rise, Happiness Is a Choice*), boils down largely to a matter of thinking. Certainly it involves deep, careful thinking, planning, and acting on the plans. Robert Schuller has written new words for the hymn tune by webb ("Stand Up for Jesus") that begin, "We build a new tomorrow on plans we make today." As Abraham Lincoln put it, "Most people are about as happy as they *make up their minds to be*" (italics ours). Author Jo Coudert has compared happiness to a cat that runs away when chased, but when you are otherwise occupied, comes and rubs up against your leg. Like money, it is the by-product of other worthwhile activity, rather than something that one seeks for itself. In

Neuro-Linguistic Programming (NLP), happiness is defined as an enhanced state of satisfaction. To be happy, then, you need only notice when you are satisfied and enhance what you are feeling at that time: be more enthusiastic, pay more attention to the details of what you are satisfied with, don't take it for granted. This is another way of saying that what you give your attention to grows.

Having free will means that we have the power to choose our behaviors—our thinking, acting, and feeling. Because of this, we are responsible for the ways that our lives are going. If we won't assume responsibility for being where we are today, we abdicate or embalm our power to determine where we'll be in the future. Many people take this to mean that they are to blame. But blame is a useless, negative emotion that just paralyzes us. We are what we say we are. If we say that we are victims, we are writing VICTIM on our own foreheads. Responsibility isn't blaming the victim; it is giving the victim a ticket out. It says that we have the power to change our circumstances because we have the power to change our minds. If we're being carried down the rapids in a rowboat, we can lie down and moan that we are about to crash into the rocks, or we can take responsibility by sitting up and steering. Psychiatrist Viktor Frankl, when held in a Nazi concentration camp under horrible conditions, discovered that he still had the power to choose his thoughts.

New Thought and Prosperity

Our thoughts about money and prosperity in general create prosperity or poverty in our lives. Studies have shown no correlation between overall prosperity and education, family background, age, heredity, or anything but attitude. You can always find an example of someone with a limitation equal to or more serious than the one you are facing who has prospered in spite of that limitation. All of us have known, or known about, people from humble backgrounds, or of limited education or intelligence, or with other apparent handicaps, who have become very wealthy. And perhaps easiest to understand is the correlation between attitude, or habitual thinking, and ability to form and sustain good relationships. What you believe about the opposite sex, or bosses, or family affects your relationships with them.

One important step toward prosperous thinking is removing unconscious negative beliefs you may have about money. Maybe you grew up in a family that thought of money as dirty, or believed that rich people lacked integrity or spirituality. How about "Money doesn't grow on trees," or the oft-misquoted "Money is the root of all evil" (It's the *love* of money that is the root of all evil, as St. Paul said in 1 Tim. 6:10). An associate of Napoleon Hill named Foster Hibbard used to describe his preacher grandfather thundering about money as the root of all evil, then taking up the collection. The young Hibbard surmised that they must do something to that money out back after the service to make it all right again, because he noticed how happy his grandfather always was with a large collection.

The truth about money is that, along with the rest of God's creation, it is inherently good but can be misused. God is our Source, and our Source can reach us through many channels. In our society, money is a necessity, and God has many channels available for taking care of our needs, if we are open to those channels. But we tend to overrely on one channel and then get upset if it closes. Part of developing a prosperity consciousness is learning to remember that God, not any one channel, is our Source.

This is particularly true at this time in our culture, when we are undergoing a paradigm shift from a manufacturing society to an information society. There will be new jobs, but they won't be for the old widget welder. He or she may have to retrain or start a new career as an entrepreneur. Many people who have been fired later said that losing their job was the best thing that ever happened to them because it led to work they really loved and could grow in.

It helps to develop what in Zen is called a *beginner's mind*, one that is poor in spirit, without intellectual arrogance, teachable. The rich young ruler who came to Jesus was possessed by his possessions, which means that he was hung up on the channels, hung up on material things at the expense of the spiritual instead of understanding that his true source of wealth was God.

This is why Jesus made his famous remark about the camel going through the needle's eye. The needle's eye was a small wicket gate in the larger gate of the city, and the only way for a camel to get through it was to be unladen of all its owner's possessions. It could then wiggle through on its knees. How appropriate a metaphor for getting rid of a lot of old mental baggage, of belief in a particular job or source of wealth!

Most of us did not grow up in New Thought, so we may have inherited odd ideas about money. It is easy to forget that money is just a convenient substitute for barter. We are all interdependent, but the shoemaker may not want three chickens at the exact time that you need new shoes. We tend to endow money with a magic that it doesn't have. It is simply an agreed-upon convenience. The "magic" is simply the way the universe operates, described under the name of the law of increase, and lest we forget, "God gave the increase" (1 Cor. 3:6). An excellent illustration of this principle of increase is the enterprising youngster who asked his dad for a monthly allowance of one cent the first day, two cents the second day, four cents the third day, and so forth. This sounded good to the old man until he multiplied it out: by Day 15, Junior would receive $163.74, and by Day 30 it would be $5,368,709.12! This is more than a chuckle, it is the foundation for all of business, be it retail sales or investments.

There is also magic in the abundance of *ideas*, which is where we get the business axiom, "Find a need and fill it." A newer version of this is "Create a need and fill it", examples being the photocopier, the computer, and the fax machine. Nobody needed them before someone invented them.

If you believe the old negative ideas about money, you will attract support for those beliefs, because that is what your brain is screening for. If you believe what the wealthy believe and what Jesus taught, that is what you will attract.

Unity minister Catherine Ponder has written numerous widely popular books, among the best known of which are *The Dynamic Laws of Prosperity* and *The Prosperity Secret of the Ages*. She points out that the Bible is the world's greatest textbook on prosperity, and that Jesus lived a prosperous existence, dining with the wealthy, wearing a rare and expensive seamless garment, paying his taxes with a gold coin found in the mouth of a fish, and having his body buried in a rich man's tomb. Her writings and those of other New Thought writers stress that we are the rich children of a loving Father, which is how Jesus taught us to imagine God. (If the Father metaphor doesn't work for you, Unity minister Edwene Gaines likes to refer to God as "Big Mama," which works well, too, as long as you don't get too carried away with anthropomorphism!) We inherit all that the Father has, namely, the resources of the entire universe, including an abundance of ideas, with the best ones for us selected specifically for us by God and given by God to us. We just *think* they're our ideas! This is a prosperity consciousness, an economics of abundance. One of the best illustrations of the difference between prosperity and poverty consciousness is a remark by the late movie producer Mike Todd: "I've been broke, but I've never been poor. Being broke is a temporary situation. Being poor is a state of mind."

Traditional Christianity tends either to glorify poverty or to view prosperity as a sign of God's favor visited only on the elect few. But Jesus said, "I am come that they might have life, and that they might have it more abundantly" (John 10:10). There is nothing about lack or limitation here. Lack and limitation come from limited thinking. We can interfere with the flow of abundance into our lives, just as we can interfere with our health by negative thinking or by mistreating our bodies by failing to keep our lives in balance. There's a much-repeated story about a little girl helping her daddy water the garden and finding to her dismay no water coming out of the hose. Her father, glancing over, immediately sees the problem and tells her to take her foot off the hose! If God is everywhere present, if we are in God, then abundance, like life itself, is everywhere present, as long as we don't block the channel through which it flows.

Unity cofounder Charles Fillmore stated flatly that poverty is a sin; the Greek word translated *sin* means "missing the mark." God intends for all of his children to live abundantly. Jesus also taught that we should love one another, and it is not necessary to prosper at the expense of someone else. In an abundant universe, there is plenty for all. Despite what you may think, numerous studies have shown that competition is counterproductive, that cooperation works better in the long run for everyone. People compete because they believe that there isn't enough to go around, that they can win only if someone else loses, that life is a zero-sum game. That is belief in lack and limitation, and it tends to become a self-fulfilling prophecy.

Now, please note that this is *not* saying that the world owes us a living, so we can sit around and do nothing. But the wheel was invented by a lazy optimist. We are all here for a reason, and the quickest route to happiness is to find out what our mission is and to work toward it. God's will for us is always the highest and the best, even though it may not seem so at the time. "Have I any pleasure at all that the wicked should die? saith the Lord God: and not that he should return from his ways, and live?" (Ezek. 18:23). (*Wicked,* by the way, comes from the same root word as *bewitched,* and implies that the person is under some sort of spell, quite possibly self-induced.) Our notions about God continued to evolve all through the writing of the Old Testament, so that it seems as if God changed his mind a lot during that time, visiting the sins of the fathers upon the children to the third and the fourth generations in Exodus, then repealing all that in the eighteenth chapter of Ezekiel. Similarly, our understanding of "Thy will be done," as Jesus offered in the Lord's Prayer as a model for us, needs another look. God's will is always for us to become the highest and best that we can be, with our natural talents and positive passions enhanced and put to work in the service of others, whether we're serving hamburgers, or gas and oil, or people's intellectual, emotional, or spiritual needs.

Financial difficulties, relationship difficulties, or any other problems can be healed, just as bodies are healed, by changing our thinking. This is the sort of statement that makes materialists go ballistic, but in view of the evidence of the new physics and the research on the effects of thoughts on blood chemistry, it is unquestionably, if uncomfortably, true. Uncomfortably, because we have nowhere to hide: who's putting all those thoughts of lack and limitation into our minds? They may have originated with mother or Diet Rite or Professor Gurmflunernge or the *Today* show, but we continue to entertain them.

Divine Science minister Emmet Fox wrote a widely circulated pamphlet titled *The Golden Key*, in which he states that the key to getting out of any difficulty is to get your mind off of the problem and onto the various aspects of God: Life, Love, Truth, Intelligence, Spirit, Soul, and Principle. (Fox believed that God, like the Capitol in Washington, is so big that we can look only at one side of him at a time.) To do this is to change your thinking from lack and limitation to abundance. Lack and limitation are thoughts that can be unthought and replaced with better thoughts.

Babies are born with very few behaviors. All other behaviors are learned. If learned, they can be unlearned, replaced with more useful behaviors. Psychiatrist William Glasser refers to *depressing* rather than depression, to indicate that on some level we are choosing that behavior. Similarly, we may choose headaching, or even heart attacking. Obviously, such behaviors are not consciously chosen: nobody wakes up in the morning and says, "Hi ho, I think I'll be depressed today." But were you born with a headache, or depressed? Still, it is useless to blame yourself for choosing a particular behavior. Anyone else in your circumstances, with your background, probably would have made similar choices. The point is to get your attention and your creative power onto what you want—in all areas of your life, not just the area that hurts at the moment.

New Thought in Business

New Thought teachings such as these quickly found their way into the business world. Unity used to publish a magazine titled *Good Business*. Napoleon Hill, a newspaperman of humble background, undertook a famous twenty-year study of highly successful people in business and politics, at the instigation of steel magnate Andrew Carnegie. Carnegie gave him encouragement and introductions, but no money; yet Hill ended up a multimillionaire. His study led him straight to New Thought principles. Journalist Claude Bristol (*The Magic of Believing*), Dale Carnegie

(*How to Win Friends and Influence People*), James Allen (*As a Man Thinketh*), and poets Ella Wheeler Wilcox and Edwin Markham were among numerous writers either active in New Thought or influenced by it.

Around the turn of the century New Thoughter and successful businessman Orison Swett Marden established *Success* magazine, revived in recent years by insurance magnate and Positive Mental Attitude (PMA) promoter W. Clement Stone, a disciple of Napoleon Hill. Then as now, it deals with what are essentially New Thought principles for succeeding in business and in life. It frequently features life stories of people who have succeeded against enormous and daunting challenges of every sort: physical, financial, political, interpersonal. The emphasis is on the power of the mind: one's beliefs, coupled with a clear vision of what one wants, backed up by the strength of character to keep on keeping on and to be of service to others in some way. It's hard to scoff at multimillionaire successes who have done the impossible and/or come back from incredible setbacks. Businessmen and best-selling authors such as Robert Ringer, Anthony Robbins, and Charles J. Givens went from rags to riches and back to rags repeatedly before they learned how to make prosperity stay around on a consistent basis. None of them makes any mention of New Thought, although Tony Robbins occasionally quotes Emmet Fox or Orison Swett Marden. It doesn't matter what you call it as long as you live by it.

New Thought in Church

Numerous clergy of various denominations have adapted New Thought teachings for their congregations, or at least read its literature for inspiration and sermon ideas. Without doubt the two strongest purveyors of New Thought principles outside the movement itself have been Reformed Church ministers Norman Vincent Peale (1898–1993) and his disciple Robert Schuller. Peale has acknowledged in print his enormous debt to New Thought in his life and ministry, and Schuller is reputed to have remarked to some New Thought ministers at his Institute for Successful Church Leadership, "You talk about it; I do it." Both

Peale and Schuller deal with peace of mind, health of body, harmonious relationships, and abundant successful living now. Both have their critics, the most famous of whom, Adlai Stevenson, announced that he found Paul appealing, but he found Peale appalling. Schuller's critics are fond of noting that the Crystal Cathedral is right down the road from Disneyland. But, critics notwithstanding, both have had enormous success personally and in their ability to help others achieve success (i.e., health, wealth, and happiness) in their own lives. And Jesus said, "By their fruits ye shall know them" (Matt. 7:20).

Just as in healing, New Thought is rich with anecdotal evidence of fortunes changed, relationships saved, and lives turned around. New Thoughters are fond of affirmations such as, "I am the rich child of a loving Father, so I dare to prosper now" and "The Christ in me salutes the Christ in you." Rather than viewing Jesus as the first and last member of the Christ family, many New Thoughters believe that Christ is a title that we can all earn by following Jesus' example. *Christ* may refer to the activity of the superconscious mind or (in process terms) the presence of God as the initial aim of each experience (see chapter 6). Organizations such as Silent Unity and the Ministry of Prayer in the United Church of Religious Science maintain telephone prayer lines for people in need of any kind, and many miracles have been reported by grateful users.

Many New Thought churches and centers hold workshops on prosperity. In these, people not only learn how to develop a prosperity consciousness, but pray (or as many say, "treat") with each other many times with amazing results. But simply to ask for something is not enough. We must change our habitual thinking into an *expectation* of attaining *and retaining* prosperity, healing, or harmony; or even if we win the lottery, the money will vanish as quickly as it came. Brian Tracy, a self-made multimillionaire and motivational speaker/writer, tells a true story of a man who won $100,000 in a lottery. At the time, he was living in an old mobile home and had seven children. Everyone was delighted at the good fortune of a really needy recipient. A year later, a newspaper reporter hunted the man up to learn just how his life had changed with his extraordinary good luck. The man was back in the mobile home, he had eight children now, and he couldn't remember what he had done with the $100,000! If you fail to plan, you plan to fail. Jesus said, "What things soever ye desire when ye pray, believe that ye receive them and ye shall have them" (Mark 11:24). He also told the parable of the foolish virgins, who failed to plan; and of the steward who buried his lord's talent (money) in the ground instead of putting it to work and was cast into outer darkness for his cynicism.

This is just as true of healing. Jesus said to the newly healed former cripple at the pool of Bethesda, "Sin no more, lest a worse thing come unto thee" (John 5:14), meaning that the man had to change his thinking *and keep it changed,* or he would find himself ill again. We have evidence in the Bible of the man's limited consciousness: his helpless attitude when he said to Jesus, "Sir, I have no man, when the water is troubled, to put me into the pool" (John 5:7). Our lifestyle, too, is a result of our beliefs. How many people neglect their bodies in terms of rest, proper food, and exercise, and steep their minds in negativity and worry thoughts, then wonder why they get sick! It's easy to make fun of Pollyanna or the Little Engine That Could ("I think I can, I think I can"), but that is what works.

People are always hungry for hope and encouragement instead of blame and shame, so New Thought has continued to grow and flourish since its early days. One of the best-known figures in New Thought who gained recognition outside the movement was Emmet Fox (1886–1951), a successful electrical engineer from London with a Roman Catholic background, who found an old metaphysical text on New Thought, became interested, moved to America, was ordained a Divine Science minister, and attracted overflow crowds to large auditoriums for his lectures in New York City in the thirties and forties. Fox spoke and wrote with wit and with such exceptional clarity that even a child could understand what he was saying. His writings have been widely used by Alcoholics Anonymous, especially before it developed its own literature. These writings worked well with AA's belief in the need to trust and turn to a higher power, to develop one's spirituality without getting involved in the elaborate dogmas of a particular religion. Fox was particularly noteworthy for his symbolic interpretation of the Bible in such books as *The Sermon on the Mount* and *The Ten Commandments.* Many who have read Emmet Fox's writings have had no idea they were reading New Thought.

Today, as New Thought is expanding, it is expressed not only indirectly in other groups, but in its own organizations, running the gamut from large city churches to small rural study groups. Some organizations are run as churches, and some function as centers. Some, such as Unity, are close to traditional Christianity in their emphasis on Jesus and in their form of worship. Others, such as Seicho-No-Ie, an organization that flourishes in Japan, pay much less attention to Jesus. But all share the belief in one Presence and one Power, and that Power is good.

5

*

New Thought and New Age

New What?

*A*nyone who hasn't been living in a cave for the last few decades knows that there is something called New Age. But comparatively few people have ever heard of New Thought. It is therefore not surprising that, among those who have heard of both groups, the two are frequently confused. To add to the confusion, New Thought has to a considerable extent nurtured New Age and is one of the many roots from which it springs. Both New Thought and New Age have ancient roots, and they both share some more recent roots. Many people can be classified as belonging to both movements.

New Age most commonly refers to the dawning of the Age of Aquarius, as in the song from the musical *Hair*. As a movement, it seemed to burst into our national consciousness about the time that *Hair* first began scandalizing people with its on-stage nudity in 1968. Tradition, or at least astrology, held that the onset of the new age would be marked by upheaval before "harmony and understanding" prevailed. Two national leaders were assassinated in that year, actors were taking their clothes off in public, and many conservatives were sure that the end of the world must be at hand. Suddenly, talk of transformation was everywhere, and numerous writers began to use the term *New Age*.

Even some sophisticated surveyors of civilization know little or nothing of New Thought as distinguished from New Age, despite the fact that as a movement, New Thought is older than New Age, dating from the last half of the nineteenth century, while the beginning of New Age often is placed in the late 1960s. Michael D'Antonio, in *Heaven on Earth: Dispatches from America's Spiritual Frontier,* fails to distinguish New Age from New Thought when he puts Science of Mind (Religious Science) into New Age.

Another example: in their 1990 book *Megatrends 2000,* John Naisbitt and Patricia Aburdene, with no mention of New Thought, refer to "the national Unity Church [as] about the closest thing to organized religion in which the eclectic modern New Ager could feel comfortable." After referring to Unity's centennial in 1989, its five hundred ministries, and the combined three million circulation of its *Daily Word* and *Unity,* the authors continue, "The Unity Church avoids the New Age label, while embracing both Jesus as the Christ and reincarnation."

A recent Unity pamphlet makes clear the distinction between Unity and New Age. It states:

> The term "New Age" refers to a non-homogeneous mixture of attitudes, beliefs, concerns, fads, and theories that constitute the thinking of a wide spectrum of people. It includes a new interest in ancient Eastern religions, yoga, and meditation; a revival of interest in spiritualism, but with the new name of channeling; and the practice of astrology, graphology, phrenology, palmistry, and numerology. For those who believe in reincarnation, the New Age includes the exploration of previous lives through past-life readings. Some New Age Thinkers also study tarot cards, out-of-body experiences, Kirlian photography, automatic writing, healing with crystals, and more.

The pamphlet concludes:

> Unity certainly does not conform with many of the teachings that have been grouped under the name of

"New Age." But many thousands of individuals have found that by following Unity's teachings, they have entered a new age of rich, meaningful living.

The International New Thought Alliance has taken a similar stand in relation to certain aspects of New Age, stating in its general information brochure, "INTA does not promote or engage in spiritualism, channeling or occult phenomena."

New Age ideas were initially welcomed by many New Thought groups; however, in recent years, major New Thought organizations have sought to distance themselves from the New Age emphasis on the occult, which traditionally has been discouraged in New Thought. New Thought emphasizes the mystical over the occult, but from the days of Quimby proto-New Thought and New Thought have been enriched by leaders who were interested in and gifted in both directions. Even mysticism is often accompanied by visions and other essentially occult phenomena, so no complete separation is possible. To a growing extent, New Thought groups find themselves in competition with New Age for lecture audiences and book purchases.

There is much more to New Age than nudity, upheaval, and the occult. Unlike New Thought, which is fairly homogeneous, the New Age movement consists of so many widely differing elements that it is difficult to describe. Many people, particularly scientists, who could be classified properly as New Age, would be horrified to be labeled or identified as such. The New Age stereotype of the kooky hippie/beatnik with ethnic apparel and a passion for such aspects of the occult as crystals and channeling may not represent the majority of those involved in the movement, the largest segment of which probably consists of those interested in various aspects of holistic healing.

Experts such as scholar of American religions J. Gordon Melton have pointed out that, as is often claimed about New Thought, there is little or nothing new about New Age. Most of its interests—occult practices, alternative healing methods, scientific discoveries—have accompanied Christianity (despite discouragement from the church) through the centuries, flowered at the time of the Enlightenment, and have slowly begun to shed the superstitions of the Middle Ages, many of which still cling to them. For this reason, New Age includes a large and significant interest in some of the cutting-edge discoveries of science, particularly physics.

Arguably the most representative statement about New Age is Marilyn Ferguson's *The Aquarian Conspiracy.* Published in 1980, it was ignored or rejected by academics and pounced on by fundamentalist Christians as evidence of a Satanic conspiracy to undermine traditional Christianity. Yet as Ferguson herself pointed out, *"conspire* literally means 'to breathe together,'" and refers to a leaderless network of people with a common interest in personal and planetary transformation, pursued from within their various walks of life. She recognized this conspiracy as indicative of a paradigm shift in our entire society, a shift for the better and with benevolent intentions.

Ferguson traces the numerous roots of New Age to "the myths and metaphors, the prophecy and poetry of the past." Numerous figures, mostly in the nineteenth and early twentieth centuries, had "premonitions of transformation." These range from Meister Eckhart, a fourteenth-century German mystic, to psychologist Abraham Maslow and anthropologist Gregory Bateson in this century. She describes the formation of networks of academics, networks of humanistic lawyers, networks of "maverick theologians."

> In the late 1970s the circles began closing rapidly. The networks overlapped, linked. There was an alarming, exhilarating conviction that something significant was coming together.

The growth and development of computers and computer networks, another aspect of New Age, made much of this networking possible.

What's in a Name?

Both New Thought and New Age have been labeled *cults.* If one defines a cult as a fundamentalist might, in terms of denying the deity of Jesus, displaying antisocial or neurotic behavior, and threatening the basic values and cultural norms of society at large, the label is unfair and inaccurate for both movements. However, Christianity was initially regarded as a cult, and *cult* can mean a religious group that has not yet matured into a fully developed religion. Authoritarian control of members is one of the characteristics often associated with cults and is inapplicable to either New Thought or New Age, with the possible exception of a few groups on the fringe of New Age. (Sometimes cult leaders—and politicians and movie stars—are referred to as charismatic; one should be careful to distinguish this meaning of charismatic, as having personal magnetism inspiring popular devotion, from the original meaning, relating to gifts of the Holy Spirit, including healing, referred to in chapter 3.)

New Age should not be confused with the *new religions,* a term that scholars of religion use to refer to some religions that may be more than a century old and are adaptations of standard brands of religion around the planet. *New religious movement* has been used to refer to groups that were new in the 1960s and 1970s; to some extent it has replaced the term *cult,* with its negative connotations. Perhaps New Age belongs within *new religious movement,* but New Age is so broad that it goes beyond the category of religion. New Age is an orientation that may better be called spiritual, although it is also occult and nutritional and therapeutic in nonreligious and nonspiritual ways.

Old and New New Age

Before attempting further descriptions of New Age, it may be helpful to propose a distinction between the broader (older) and narrower (current) meanings of New Age. New Thoughters since the early days of the movement have been proclaiming a New Age. Evans wrote of the New Age, and Hopkins referred to "a new song for the hearts of the Children of the New Age." In the 1930s one of the most popular New Thought authors and speakers, Emmet Fox, was writing of our having entered the enlightened Age of Aquarius that was traditionally expected to follow the dark and violent Age of Pisces. One of the early

New Thoughters expressed surprise that the Spanish-American War had taken place, since there had been such a great turn-around in thought by 1898!

In this broad sense of the New Age—promoting a new, more practical, down-to-earth peaceful, spiritual perspective and style of life—New Thought is not only a part of the New Age—but its very core. It was the pioneer in the most practical and Western-oriented sides of New Age thinking and techniques for healing of mind, body, and circumstances. It is the part of this broader approach to living that has become a stable feature of religion and holds the greatest hope for becoming a systematized outlook consistent with basic Western religious and philosophical insights. New Thought shows signs of becoming a self-critical, evolving philosophico-spiritual nucleus around which more rational New Agers and others could come together.

However, many New Agers might not choose to unite in even such a loosely organized entity as New Thought. D'Antonio emphasizes the blending of New Age and whatever religion one already has. New Age is unlike religions that demand exclusive loyalty from their adherents. New Agers pick and choose as they like from New Age "ideas about health, politics, psychology, or spirituality" while retaining their already established religious identity. "They become New Age Catholics who wear crystals, or New Age Jews who consult psychics."

Proto–New Age: the "Metaphysical" Family

Commentators on New Age have endeavored to find the origins of New Age and have done a good job, but they seem not to have realized clearly that the combination of these sources in the nineteenth century and first half of the twentieth century already constituted a proto–New Age. To be sure, it was not so widespread nor influential nor so self-aware of its various aspects as constituting one amorphous movement.

What we are calling the *metaphysical family*, which constituted proto–New Age or the Old New Age, includes at least the groups dealt with in J. Stillson Judah's *The History and Philosophy of the Metaphysical Movements in America*. In this Judah considers not only New Thought, Christian Science, and Pealeistic positive thinking, but also Spiritualism and Theosophy and its allies, the Arcane School, and the Astara Foundation. One might even extend the metaphysical family back to the first half of the nineteenth century and include its utopian communities, channeling, and alternative healing.

As we have already lamented, the term *metaphysical* is an unfortunate one to apply to any group or groups, partly because it does not distinguish among views about the nature of reality. One religion is as much founded on some metaphysical position as is any other. As popularly used, it also implies a concern with a realm beyond or in addition to the physical, whereas traditional metaphysics seeks to explain both the seen and the unseen on the basis of some reality that may or may not be different from what our usual senses reveal to us.

Some terminological help, as well as a pointing toward New Age, comes from Sydney E. Ahlstrom. In *A Religious History of the American People* he uses the term *harmonial religion* to refer to New Thought, Christian Science, and the positive thinking most associated with Norman Vincent Peale. Ahlstrom defines harmonial religion as:

> those forms of piety and belief in which spiritual composure, physical health, and even economic well-being are understood to flow from a person's rapport with the cosmos. Human beatitude and immortality [?] are believed to depend to a great degree on one's being "in tune with the infinite" [the title of the famous nearly century-old best-seller by Ralph Waldo Trine].

Ahlstrom sees harmonial religion as

> a vast and highly diffuse religious impulse that cuts across all normal lines of religious division. It often shapes the inner meaning of the church life to which people formally commit themselves. . . . Some of its motifs probably inform the religious life of most Americans. During the 1960s [the book was published in

1972], moreover, one could note a steady growth in the strength of this general impulse, while closely related but more esoteric forms of religion [of occult and Eastern types] . . . seemed to thrive even more vigorously.

In the last sentence Ahlstrom was concerned with what later would be known as New Age.

Despite the availability of *harmonial religion,* it seems unlikely that the term *metaphysical religion* will fade away, partly because it has been used to cover a wider range of outlooks than Ahlstrom included in *harmonial religion.*

New Age Demographics

D'Antonio reports a University of California at Santa Barbara estimate that as many as twelve million Americans are actively involved in New Age and another thirty million highly interested. He adds that if they were united in a church, it would be the third largest denomination in the country.

An impressive aspect of New Age is the wealth and influence of its adherents. More than 90 percent of the subscribers to *New Age Journal* are college graduates, and they are "three times more likely than others to travel abroad and four times more likely to be active in politics or community affairs." In summary, they

> tend to be educated, affluent and successful people. They are hungry for something mainstream society has not given them. . . . They don't care for existing religions, so they've come out with a new kind of religion. . . .
>
> The New Age arose in part, because those who leave the structure of mainstream religion nonetheless retain the basic human need for community, ritual, and spiritual expression. . . .
>
> They are the experimenters, the theorizers, the explorers who will defy convention and chart their own routes to fulfillment.

D'Antonio observes that New Age concerns about "meditation, mind-body theories, staunch environmentalism, visualization can be found in public schools, hospitals, corporate offices, and the popular media." One gets the impression that one scarcely can take a breath without absorbing something of New Age. To be, and especially to be young, in the closing years of the twentieth century is to be, to some degree, a New Ager. New Age ideas are "leeching into the larger society, where they are being adopted by people who would never identify themselves as part of the movement."

A Scripps Howard News Service story by Terry Mattingly was published in April 1994 with the title "New Age on way to being old hat." In the article, Russell Chandler, author of *Understanding the New Age,* is quoted as saying that New Age faith "has become so visible that it's now all but invisible. . . . Now, New Age has gone mainstream." Mattingly notes that

> Revelations about crystals, channeling and pyramids are on the decline, or at least less public. Today the emphasis is on angels and all-forgiving images of eternal light. . . . The fads have faded. But key New Age principles are now part of the cultural landscape.

New Age Interests and Activities

D'Antonio finds New Agers' prime interests to be spiritual healing, environmentalism, and paranormal phenomena (from ESP to spirit channeling to UFOs). He characterizes New Age as

> a very flexible, amorphous, spontaneous movement. There is no national organization, no hierarchy, no clearinghouse for information. People become part of the movement by studying books, visiting small institutes, joining study groups, attending seminars, and working with the thousands of New Age therapists, teachers, healers, and gurus scattered around the country. A typical believer draws on these different interests

to create his own, personal way of thinking about himself and the world around him.

As already seen, New Age incorporates much of earlier times, including nineteenth-century American utopian communities, channeling, and alternative healing.

D'Antonio notes similarities between New Age and Charismatic Christian churches, which have roughly the same number of adherents as New Age. Although New Agers consider Christians "authoritarian, dogmatic, stultifying, and, in the end, spiritually damaging" and conservative Christians consider New Agers "atheistic, occultist, evil," and in the service of the devil, these two opposing camps share interests in "right living, a personal connection to God, an apocalyptic sense of the future, metaphysical healing, spiritual renewal."

Also emphasizing the communitarian side of New Age and its belief in divine immanence is Mary Farrell Bednarowski in her 1989 book, *New Religions and the Theological Imagination in America*. She finds two particular characteristics of New Age: (1) spiritual communities pointing toward "emerging planetary culture" and individual spiritual transformation, all founded on (2) the immanence of divinity. She observes:

> Depending on the particular group, the concept of immanence may find expression in an occult or Eastern world view reminiscent of Theosophy. Or, it may take form within the framework of a Roman Catholic or Anglican understanding of the sacramental nature of reality and of the relationship between the spiritual and material worlds. Whatever the origins of their immanentist cosmologies, New Age theorists have in common a perception of this particular time in history as one of drastic change—paradigmatic change—that will affect all the institutions of the culture, not just organized religion.

She stresses that the New Age opposition to a dualism that sharply "separates spirit from matter, male from female, body from soul, science from religion, reason from feeling" leads to emphasis on "wholeness—individual, communal, national, and planetary." Bednarowski notes that although Christian New Age groups, such as that of Matthew Fox, "do not speak of spirit guides, they nonetheless offer instruction in a variety of techniques for seeking the divine within such as meditation, yoga, massage, and fasting."

After noting that New Age ideas do not seem very new to anyone familiar with Theosophy and nineteenth-century Spiritualism, she distinguishes current New Age from older manifestations of the same overall outlook as follows:

> First, the application of New Age concepts to contemporary issues of a global nature, such as ecology, world hunger, and, particularly concerns about nuclear warfare and world peace, all of which have implications for the formation of a planetary culture; and, second, the broadening of a concept of immanence from one which must necessarily be tied to an occult or Eastern world view . . . to one that allows one to be a Christian.

She notes that New Age thought continues much of Theosophy's emphases on universal brotherhood, comparative religion, philosophy and science, and unfolding of the supersensory powers of people.

Summing up what we have seen so far, New Age represents a confluence of interests in the occult, apocalyptic events, personal and planetary healing and transformation, scientific advances, and Eastern philosophy and religion. Individual New Agers pick and choose in varying proportions from this smorgasbord of concerns, and by no means do they agree about or share an interest in all of them.

But Will It Last?

Experts disagree as to whether New Age is here to stay. New Thought minister and scholar Dell de Chant believes that some parts of New Age eventually will become institutionalized and remain. Melton believes that New Age is essentially a revivalist movement that, after accomplishing its mission, will dissolve back into its various streams of interest. On the other hand, in "New Thought and the New Age," in Lewis and Melton (eds.) *Perspectives on the New Age*, Melton classifies New Thought as having been established from the beginning as "a new and separate religious movement [that has] subsequently grown into a distinct religious family tradition analogous to the Lutherans or the Baptists." In support of this, Phillip C. Lucas, in *Perspectives on the New Age*, has pointed out that, like Pentecostal/Charismatics, New Agers seek to empower, heal, and transform the individual, possibly as part of a Great Awakening, comparable to that which many believe characterized eighteenth-century America.

Catherine L. Albanese's *Nature Religion in America* provides a helpful perspective from which to view both New Thought and New Age. She relates them to varying attitudes that Americans have had toward nature, from Amerindian to ecofeminist. She observes that today "Transcendentalists prosper in the general harmonial-metaphysical dialectic of New Age religion and in the special case of Goddess religion." Albanese links current Transcendentalists with quantum physics in an attempt to solve problems of the nature of nature and whether our attitudes toward nature should be those of conquest or harmony.

Similarities Between New Age and New Thought

New Thought and New Age both believe in a direct relationship with the Ultimate, however conceived. Neither movement favors hierarchical organizations, and both groups treat women and men as partners, with many women in leadership roles. Many people in both groups believe in reincarnation, because they feel that we can't learn all we need to learn in one lifetime.

New Age, like New Thought, is strongly optimistic, largely because most people in both groups believe in a good God, and that all people are part of God or have at least a spark of the divine. New Agers are full of hope for the transformation of society and the planet. New Thought accepts, as does New Age, the old Hermetic teaching, "As above, so below," which appears in an early version of the Lord's Prayer as "As in heaven, so on earth" (Luke 11:2). Heaven, in a New Thought interpretation, alludes to one's state of mind, and earth is the manifestation of that state. As in mind, so in manifestation. Symbolically interpreted, heaven is the uplifted state of consciousness, the wonderful, peaceful sense of universal oneness that the mystic seeks. Charles Fillmore defines it as "a state of consciousness in which the soul and the body are in harmony with Divine Mind." All of Jesus' metaphors about heaven are attempts to explain the necessity for disciplining our thoughts, weeding out the negative ones and treasuring the positive ones; e.g., the pearl of great price, tares growing with the wheat, seeds falling in various places with various results. New Age shares New Thought's interest in metaphor, and the late Joseph Campbell, the preeminent authority on myth and metaphor, is a popular New Age author.

In large part borrowing from or paralleling New Thought, New Agers generally believe that there is only one Presence and Power in the universe and that that Power is good (although there may be a small segment who believe in Satan). Many see that Power as both immanent and transcendent. Both movements have a growing interest in panentheism (not to be confused with the old heresy, pantheism, which holds that God and the universe are one), expounded on at length by one of us (Alan) in New Thought and with perhaps a somewhat different understanding by former Roman Catholic and now Episcopal priest Matthew Fox, in New Age. The word *panentheism* may be reflected by another Roman Catholic priest, Teilhard de Chardin, in his favorite passage of Scripture, *"En pasi panta Theon"* (that God may be all in all). It is the idea that all is in God, rather than the more limited pantheist notion that God is all. "In Him we live and move and have our being" (Acts 17:28). New Thoughters frequently affirm, "There is no place where God is not," a neat paraphrase of Psalm 139. Teilhard, whose works were suppressed by the Roman Catholic church during his lifetime, is frequently regarded as one of the fathers of New Age, according to a survey conducted by Marilyn Ferguson.

Like New Thought, New Age also emphasizes the value of

meditation. Much of this interest springs from the influence of Eastern religions on both movements, as well as the importance given to the power of the mind and the necessity for disciplining or training the mind.

New Thought and New Age both frequently seek alternatives to orthodox medicine, especially in overlooked natural and scientific discoveries for healing that lack the huge profit potential of drugs or surgery. Members of both groups use orthodox medicine when it is appropriate but seek better choices where it falls short or fails altogether. They particularly seek to learn to harness the power of the mind to heal, and increasing amounts of scientific research have supported this approach. New Age physician Larry Dossey in his most recent book, *Healing Words,* has listed over a hundred studies on the power of prayer to heal, over half showing that prayer brings about "significant changes." The result of one randomized, double-blind study by a cardiologist was so significant that Dossey states, "If the technique studied had been a new drug or a surgical procedure instead of prayer, it would almost certainly have been heralded as some sort of 'breakthrough.'" Dossey also describes three eras in medicine: Era I, physicalistic medicine, dominant from the 1860s to 1950 and "still influential"; Era II, mind-body medicine, arising in the 1950s and still developing; and Era III, nonlocal science and medicine, "just being recognized."

In this, New Age is clearly building on New Thought, which began with Quimby's use of the power of the mind to heal, frequently with absent healing. Most New Age groups—and indeed, individuals—welcome New Thought teachings on healing and general prosperity, along with its views on God, once they become aware of New Thought's existence.

New Age is fascinated with the new physics, and New Thought shares this interest. Both movements are philosophically idealistic, and the findings of the new physics support idealism. Marilyn Ferguson observes, "the new science goes beyond cool, clinical observations to a realm of shimmering paradox, where our very reason seems endangered." Physicists are starting to sound like metaphysicians. Research moves so fast that results are obsolete before they can appear in print. Scientists have repeatedly demonstrated the mind's ability to affect the body, beginning with biofeedback and extending into studies showing that white blood cell count varied according to whether subjects thought happy or unhappy thoughts. Bell's Theorem led to experiments showing that paired particles remain mysteriously connected even after they fly apart, another example of the nonlocality that Dossey mentions in connection with Era III medicine. Neuroscientist Karl Pribram's research on holograms suggests that the universe may be a giant hologram—in other words, we are all one. As he puts it, "The brain we know now allows for the experiences reported from spiritual disciplines."

And Differences

But New Thought and New Age do differ, whether or not both are viewed as religions. One big difference is interest in the occult. Crystals, pyramids, and other occult trappings belong to New Age, not New Thought. Unity founders Charles and Myrtle Fillmore investigated various occult practices such as channeling early in their ministry and rejected them as largely ineffective and possibly even dangerous for dabblers. Still, New Thought does remain open to truth from whatever unlikely source it may spring. It may discourage interest in the occult, but it does not invariably condemn it.

In the early years of current New Age thinking, John Charles Cooper, in his *Religion in the Age of Aquarius*, characterized New Age interest in the occult as a wholesale rejection of a society founded on materialistic positivism (not to be confused with positive thinking). He found that this interest originated in people's frustration with social conditions that they believed they could not control. If this is so, New Age and New Thought have different psychological origins; New Thought never has suffered from a feeling of inability to deal adequately with a world held to be essentially mental and subject to mental control.

The supposedly channeled New Age work *A Course in Miracles*, purportedly coming from Jesus, remains popular among Unity churches despite efforts to discourage its use. Many people undoubtedly have been helped by the Course, especially by its emphasis on forgiveness and its discussion groups in which people share their problems, but it remains quintessentially New Age, not New Thought. New Agers Gerald Jampolsky and Marianne Williamson have mined the valuable nuggets of the Course and set them down admirably in their own writings.

New Thought does not emphasize its countercultural aspects, though it does represent something of a break with traditional Christianity. However, according to Unity minister Dell de Chant,

> Since New Thought has failed to establish practical and academic relationships with mainstream churches, and because it has neither promoted its own intellectual development nor pursued its unique spiritual horizons, it has few other sources besides the New Age to turn to for institutional inspiration and ideological refreshment.

One way of describing a significant difference between New Thought and New Age is to say that New Thought is to New Age as psychology is to sociology. One of us (Deb), as a graduate student in psychology, frequently found herself in the sociology section of the library. Psychology concentrates its attention largely on the behavior of the individual; sociology deals mainly with the behavior of groups. Groups are, of course, made up of individuals, so distinctions are frequently blurred. New Thought has been criticized—in part unfairly—for its lack of emphasis on charitable works. But to teach individuals the power of their own minds and their oneness with a good God is to obviate the need for charitable works in the long run, as the individuals become empowered to achieve on their own. There is a saying—often attributed to Abraham Lincoln—"Give a man a fish and you feed him for a day; teach a man to fish and you feed him for a lifetime." Jesus taught his followers to fish well, and there are many wonderful symbolic New Thought interpretations of these teachings; fish symbolize ideas. New Agers share this desire to empower and transform the individual, and continue their attention out to the transformation of the group and the planet as a whole. New Thoughters are frequently found with them.

New Thought comes nearer to relying exclusively on spiritual healing than does New Age. New Thought allows and sometimes even encourages use of both conventional medicine and alternative healing methods, but recognizes them as *outside* New Thought. In contrast, most if not all of the alternative forms of healing are *within* the broad boundaries of New Age.

The Ever-Present Critics

The most vociferous critics of New Age, and to a lesser extent of New Thought, are the fundamentalist evangelical Christians, who feel threatened by any departure from traditional authoritarian Christian teachings. These critics take literally the "conspiracy" metaphors applied to New Age, and see the entire movement as the work of Satan, in whom they devoutly believe. Evangelical and scholar Irving Hexham did a study comparing random passages of best-selling New Age books with some from Christian best-sellers. His results showed that New Age books on the average required a grade 14 reading level; Christian books, a grade 9 level. "Such a big discrepancy," he says, " . . . does not augur well for the future of evangelical Christianity." Hexham also points out that failure of evangelicals to define their terms frequently leads to misunderstandings. Certainly, it is always important to exercise discernment in approaching such a mixed bag as the New Age movement. But Jesus said, "By their fruits ye shall know them," and New Age has many wonderful fruits to display in terms of renewed interest in caring for God's creatures and creation, as well as individual empowerment and transformation. Many fundamentalist charges are simply inaccurate, and some are downright hysterical. Increased individual freedom is noisier and messier than lockstep authoritarian control, but it bears sweeter fruits.

These critics miss the point: we have the power to heal ourselves, our pocketbooks, and our planet, and perform other miracles *because of our relationship with God,* if we are willing to make the most of it. Jesus said, "I speak not of myself: but the Father that dwelleth in me, he doeth the works" (John 14:10).

Less severe critics include D'Antonio, who discovered much good in New Age but also found that it "lacks the depth and the social conscience of Christianity and Judaism," that it is missing the myths needed to "teach, inspire, enlighten, and unite," and fails to have "a serious commitment to service to the community at large."

Gordon Davidson and Corinne McLaughlin, in their *Spiritual Politics*, an Ageless Wisdom-oriented book, disagree:

> A new idea given to humanity in the middle of this century as a next step was the vision of group consciousness—humans transcending self-centeredness to participate consciously in groups working for the salvation of humanity. The embryonic beginnings of this awakening can be seen in the best aspects of the "New Age."

Critics of New Age or New Thought frequently appear to resent the notion that people might *enjoy* and be *aided by* their religion in this-worldly ways of health, wealth, and happiness, rather than merely comforted in the depths of their misery by the thought of pie in the sky in the sweet by-and-by. Brief therapies often encounter similar criticism from those who insist that meaningful change *must* be difficult and take a long time, even when they are presented with evidence to the contrary. But as New Thought and much of New Age can attest, our beliefs shape our experiences, not the other way around.

Summary

New Thought concentrates on the power of the mind to heal and to prosper in a world in which all is mind. New Age especially extends this healing, prospering transformation to the entire planet, and with the inquisitiveness of youth, pokes its nose into numerous interesting corners, some clearly valuable, some questionable, in the process. It is possible to share in many of these interests, beliefs, and practices, yet continue to belong to mainstream Christianity or other religions.

The success of both New Thought and New Age can be measured to a considerable extent by the degree to which their interests and teaching have seeped into cultures that neither know nor care about either group by name. By this measure, both are successful and probably will become increasingly so. It seems almost certain that New Thought will continue, largely in its current organizational ways. Many New Agers will find their way to New Thought organizations, but probably most will remain outside any organized religion or even organized spirituality. However, the world is far too complex and the changes that are occurring are far too profound to make predictions worth much. What seems clear is that with or without capital letters, we have entered a promising new age, and New Thought will remain an important and distinguishable part of it.

6

*

Something New
in New Thought

God's Job Description and Yours

Have you ever wondered what is in God's job description?
The *divine* job description provides for God to *start every-*
thing, to *finish nothing,* and to *keep everything. Your* job description
calls for you to *start nothing,* to *finish very quickly what God starts*
for you, and to realize that *you can't keep anything* for more than
a moment. If this seems to violate common sense, keep reading.

Not-So-Common Sense

It is lamentably true that common sense is uncommon. It is also
lamentably true (sorry to ruin your day) that even common
sense, much as we trust and respect it, is no longer adequate by
itself for understanding our universe. As British scientist J. B.
S. Haldane remarked, "The universe is not only stranger than
we imagine, it is stranger than we *can* imagine."

The relationship of a philosopher and a psychologist can get
prickly at times. At first, we attributed it to lack of a common
language between disciplines: we were being jarred by jargon.
If the only interdisciplinary language were mathematics, both
of us would be reduced to communicating with grunts, gestures,
and perhaps smoke signals. But we persevered, and it finally
dawned on us that psychology was attempting to use common
sense, whereas philosophy was running on insight and pure rea-

soning ability. Well, you already knew that psychology is unreasonable and philosophy makes no common sense. Still, although you don't have to be able to take the engine apart in order to drive a car, at least a few of us need to be able to tell a distributor cap from a hubcap, and a few of us need to be philosophers.

Emmet Fox said that upon entering church, you should not check your common sense at the door with your hat. He should have suggested at least occasionally checking your common sense, but not your reasoning ability or your intuitive ability.

Several decades ago, newspaper readers of Don Marquis were entertained by the antics of Archy and Mehitabel: a vers libre poet transmigrated into the body of a cockroach, and an Egyptian queen who similarly ended up as an alley cat, though always a lady. Archy, the cockroach, did the typing—and most of the serious philosophizing for the pair. And so, in the interest of reasoning ability and understanding the universe, we shall turn things over to the philosopher. As Mehitabel would say, "Whatthehell, whatthehell."

New Thought has advanced far enough beyond the limitations of common sense to recognize that the world is mind rather than matter, but most of New Thought has yet to progress to the point of understanding that mind is not a *thing* but a succession of interrelated, fleeting *events* or *happenings* or *experiences*—momentarily developing minds.

The great hope for New Thought is that it will be able to do something practically unheard of for religious, or even spiritual, organizations: to continue to grow and to adapt itself to changing ideas in a changing world. Ernest Holmes characterized Religious Science as "open at the top," and a Unity pamphlet refers to Unity as "an open-ended religion." But many New Thoughters declare that there is nothing new in New Thought, that it is a rediscovery of ancient truths and practices. Until now, New Thought has turned largely to ancient sources of inspiration and ideology, but that need not continue to be exclusively the case. New Thought has a revolutionary past and holds equally revolutionary possibilities for the future.

Paradigm Shifts: Revolutions of Thought

The most important revolutions in human history are *revolutions of understanding,* which in turn produce *revolutions in ways of liv-*

ing. Thomas Kuhn called scientific and other major intellectual revolutions *paradigm shifts.* Probably the best known of these is the Copernican revolution, which led us to realize that our planet is not the center of the universe, nor even of the solar system; sometimes any major shift of understanding is called a Copernican revolution. In some respects an even more far-reaching revolution was the shift from mythological explanations to literal ones at the start of Western philosophy and science. We could call this the *literalism revolution.*

Of greatest relevance to this book is the spiritual revolution that includes New Thought, the latest in a long line of spiritual revolutions, extending over several thousand years. Spiritual revolutions have brought significant advances in our understanding of what God is like and how to relate to God in our daily living. They have involved shifts from belief in a multiplicity of supernatural powers to a single divinity, from sacrifice to ethical living, and from fear to love. The revolution involving New Thought includes the final breakdown of the distinction drawn between sacred and secular, and the practice of the presence of God for practical purposes. The first phase of this revolution began with Quimby and was expressed in terms of traditional substance philosophy, generally with a pantheistic outlook. The second phase is beginning with a rethinking of the metaphysical foundation of New Thought, centering on process philosophy and panentheism.

In order to understand this new spiritual revolution, we need to look back at what it is replacing. It is helpful to glance briefly at the *ancient* and *medieval* outlooks and to contrast *modern* and *postmodern* outlooks.

The ancient and medieval outlooks had various competing elements, but they shared a basic approach to reality. They (and the later periods) stand in contrast to the earlier mythological, poetic, nonliteral approach to reality. This touched the heart and gave people a way of placing themselves into the context of a meaningful universe, but it was of little help in discovering literal truth. Although Christianity retains some mythological components, it employs rational thought in its theology.

We should not underestimate the importance of myths. They are not errors, lies, falsehoods; they are stories that touch people at depths that go beyond the literal. It may be that we never can fully demythologize, for demythologizing may be only remythologizing. Tillich classified myths as *unbroken myths* (unrecognized as myths, so taken literally by those who accept them) and *broken myths* (recognized as such, yet still employed). Despite the value of myths, moving beyond them was a revolution essential for the evolution of thought. Literalism as an ideal is a powerful one, even if we may fool ourselves in thinking that we can be fully literal.

Around 600 B.C., Western philosophy started asking for rational answers to basic questions. Wherever we choose to go, we carry with us this heritage of rationality. We may appreciate the mythological approach to the world, but we must enter into it as outsiders. We are no longer people born into it and taking it for granted, unnoticed, much as a deep-water fish probably is unaware that it is in water, since it knows no other environment.

The first question that philosophy asked was: What does everything comes from? What is the original or underlying reality? The philosopher Thales proposed the first answer: water. Not long afterward, philosophers suggested the other three traditional elements: air, fire, and earth, as well as the boundless or infinite, and numbers.

Soon, philosophers became concerned with the problem of how anything could become anything that it had not previously been. Heraclitus said that all is in a balanced state of flux, that change is basic, that you cannot step into the same river twice. On the other hand, Parmenides and his followers (known as Eleatics, named for the Italian city where they lived) maintained that we cannot consistently think change, so change is illusory. Strange as it may seem, changelessness won the day. The Christians, when they came along, applied changelessness to their conception of God, and only in the twentieth century have many of us realized that Heraclitus was correct. We might even say that the major scientific and philosophical theme of the past century has been the rediscovery and development of the thought of Heraclitus.

Huston Smith, in *Beyond the Post-Modern Mind,* presents the

TABLE 2

CHRISTIAN, MODERN, AND POSTMODERN VIEWS

Christian View	Modern View	Postmodern View
Reality is focused in a person.	That reality may be personal is less certain and less important than that it is ordered.	Many are no longer sure that reality is ordered and orderly. The sense of the cosmos has been shaken by an encyclopedic skepticism.
The mechanics of the physical world exceed our comprehension.	Human reason can discern this order as it manifests itself in the laws of nature.	If reality is orderly, many are not sure that the human mind is capable of grasping its order.
The way to our salvation lies not in conquering nature but in following the commandments that God has revealed to us.	The path to human fulfillment consists primarily in discovering the laws of nature, utilizing them where it is possible, and complying with them where it is not.	Perhaps there is no way of salvation or fulfillment, except for our own idiosyncratic satisfactions in the midst of a world of intellectual deconstruction.

Christian, modern, and postmodern worldviews. We have summarized and largely quoted from Smith in the Table 2 above.

In sum, postmodernism is a downer. Perhaps the most devastating statement about a postmodern outlook is Smith's observation: "For twenty-five hundred years philosophers have argued over which metaphysical system is true. For them to agree that none is, is a new departure."

Alternatives to Postmodernism: Primordialism/Perennialism

Are we left with nothing but despair in this postmodern world? Far from it! There are at least two alternatives to choose from.

The first is a return to what is called by such names as the *primordial tradition* or the *perennial philosophy* or the *ancient wisdom,* which is part of the foundation of transpersonal psychology and other New Age thinking, and is adopted by much of New Thought. Smith summarizes it in terms of:

1. A *metaphysics* maintaining that reality is arranged in tiers, with the higher levels more full of being—more real—than the lower ones. In other words, there are gradations of reality, a little bit like different grades of automotive oil, ranging from thick to thin.

2. A philosophical *psychology* claiming a similarity or identity of the soul and divine Reality. We are divine, although most of us have little or no realization of it.

3. An *ethics* emphasizing human purpose as the discovery of our place in God, with the goal not simply knowledge but a new state of being. This means that we should be aiming at personal transformation that makes the presence of the divine a living reality, rather than simply something that we affirm intellectually. Perhaps the best known repository of such an outlook is Hinduism, and we have seen that this outlook is commonly accepted in New Age circles and in much of New Thought.

A noted expositor of primordialism, Ken Wilber, emphasizes the paradoxicality of the Ultimate: it is and is not whatever one may say about it. He stresses that "all propositions about reality are void and invalid." This is very convenient if one wishes to discredit the views of one's opponents. If we were to take primordialism with full seriousness and accept the Ultimate as beyond words and reason, we would discard philosophy and say nothing about the Ultimate. But the eloquent supporters of primordialism ignore this and press on to claim that the Ultimate is impersonal, which probably tells us more about supporters of primordialism than it does about the Ultimate. From the standpoint of traditional Western thought, this is the most objectionable claim of primordialism. Theism takes a personal God to be ultimate, but primordialism claims that a personal God could be no more than an emanation or outflowing from the Ultimate.

Like other overflowings from the superabundance of the One, a personal God, subordinate to the Ultimate, never really becomes separated from the One, and is only a muddled notion of human beings who picture the Ultimate as somewhat like themselves, according to primordialism. Well, when it comes to muddled notions, they ought to know.

The Ultimate Reality of primordialism is the World Woofer, whom we have already met in the Divine Kennel. The major objection to this view that there is *nothing but* God is that it robs us of the reality of our very existence as unique, permanent perspectives within the Whole and of the significance of our choices of all sorts, especially in ethics. As part of his unsuccessful attempt to wean New Thought from pantheistic tendencies, Horatio W. Dresser wrote, in *The Arena* (1899), about the form of primordialism known as the Vedanta:

> If we say with Vivekananda, "you are all God . . . Is not the whole universe you?" what ground is left for righteous conduct, the basis of which is responsibility to a superior Power, to a high moral ideal or sense of duty? The Vedanta replies that one ought not to injure one's neighbor, because one would be injuring one's self. . . . But this is egoism. The essence, the beauty of love is *to love another,* to deny one's self for another . . . to rise above myself. It is a duty, an obligation. The existence of the moral law implies that there are at least two beings in the world. It implies that individual, ethical man really exists, not merely seems to exist; that he possesses powers of choice and will; that he acts separately; that his acts are right or wrong, not in maya, but as judged by an eternal law, or by the higher Being who imposes the obligation.

Albert C. Knudson similarly emphasized the importance of our understanding of the ethical nature of God. He maintained that religion is "primarily interested in his ethical character":

> The bare absoluteness of God might awaken the sense of wonder and his metaphysical personality might elicit

a spirit of inquiry with reference to the ultimate meaning of life; but these mental states belong only to the ante-chamber of religion. In its essence religion is trust in the goodness of God. If God were a nonmoral Being, either intelligent or nonintelligent, he would not be a proper object of religious faith. It is only insofar as he is morally good, and so worthy of being trusted, that he is truly God in the religious sense of the term. . . .

Faith in the responsiveness of the superworld to human need has always been the heart of religion, and the development of religion through the ages has consisted largely in the increasing clearness and thoroughness with which men have moralized this responsiveness. . . . The biblical revelation was in its essential and distinctive nature a revelation of the moral character of God, a revelation of his righteousness and love, or, in the broader sense of the term, a revelation of his goodness.

Getting Personal

Many major philosophers and religionists regard *personhood* as the key to understanding everything. Personalism is a major form of idealism, associated primarily with Borden Parker Bowne (1845–1910) and his successors. Charles Hartshorne, who is not usually classified as a personalist, says that "personality is the only principle of wholeness, of integration, on a complex level such as the universe must involve, of which we have any experience."

Person does not always mean *human being*. As personalist philosopher Edgar S. Brightman puts it,

> A *person* is a self that is potentially self-conscious, rational, and ideal. That is to say, when a self is able at times to reflect on itself as a self, to reason, and to acknowledge ideal goals by which it can judge its actual achievements, then we call it a person.

All normal human beings are persons, but not all persons are human beings. If certain animals, such as dolphins and whales, are as advanced as we are led to believe, they may be persons; if there are angels, presumably they are persons. There may be many kinds of nonhuman persons inhabiting planets throughout the universe. Above all other persons is the ultimate Person, God, personal not only in relation to us, but in him/herself. God is the only complete Person; we are fragmentary persons. There is no impersonal Ultimate beyond or underlying the personal God.

We emphasize that *person* and *personal* as used here do not refer to one's more or less superficial mask (what the words literally refer to) or guise or public role covering one's deeper character or individuality, but to that basic individuality itself.

To some it seems conceited and unduly human being–centered (anthropocentric) to think that something more like us than like a rock (which is about as impersonal a thing as you can imagine) could be the highest reality. But ask yourself whether you can conceive of the highest, most basic, originating reality as something lacking in individuality (unity), self-consciousness, self-control, rationality, wisdom, love, ethical sensitivity, sense of humor, ability to choose one course of action rather than another, appreciation of beauty. Can you believe that a reality having such qualities is dependent on anything lacking them, or arose out of such a dull existence? To believe that it, or we, could have done so is to embrace a materialism that dispenses with anything worthy of being called God. Albert C. Knudson corrected a common misplacement of God and ourselves when he noted, "In emphasizing the personality of God we affirm, not the likeness of God to man, but rather the likeness of man to God." Borden Parker Bowne maintains that "complete and perfect personality can be found only in the Infinite and Absolute Being, as only in Him can we find that complete and perfect selfhood and self-possession which are necessary to the fullness of personality." Bowne warns against

> transferring to [the Supreme Person] the limitations and accidents of our human personality, which are *no necessary* part of the notion of personality, and think

only of the fullness of power, knowledge, and selfhood which alone are the essential factors of the conception.

Alternatives to Postmodernism: What's Behind Door #2?

If we find *person* to be the ultimate explanatory category, where shall we turn to understand most adequately how reality works? We can, of course, turn back to old notions of a God fashioned anthropomorphically as including most, if not all, human shortcomings. However, we don't recommend that. Instead, we can look ahead to something relatively new and splendid, sophisticated enough to satisfy anyone, yet simple enough in its broad outlines to be understood by most questing people.

We are betting on the basic insights of what is known as *process philosophy* (or *process thought* or *process theology*—or *process-relational philosophy*, to emphasize the interrelatedness of everything in the universe), or *positive postmodernism* (in contrast to most postmodernism, which is decidedly negative). By whatever name we call it, it is the major alternative to the primordial tradition, while sharing with primordialism recognition of the centrality of a spiritual approach to life. Process philosophy has become so important that there has been established a Center for Process Studies affiliated with the Claremont Graduate School and the School of Theology at Claremont, California.

Process philosophy is based on a few obvious facts: (1) the world is changing, developing; (2) everything is related to everything else; (3) we can live only in the moment, and have to deal with everything in little chunks of time and space. If we also believe (4) that there is a divine guiding intelligence that enters into our lives, and that (5) memories and other influences from the past also play important roles in contributing to what we are, we have practically embraced process thought, although we may never have heard of it.

Although process philosophy has ancient (including Buddhist) and turn-of-the-present-century roots, it is primarily the product of the insights of Alfred North Whitehead (1861–1947) and Charles Hartshorne (born in 1897). One important source on which they drew is twentieth-century science, which has abandoned belief in enduring substance. Whitehead recognized that although physics was correct in explaining the world in terms of bursts of energy, physics was missing an essential ingredient by considering energy to be lifeless. Process philosophy emphasizes that *living* events, happenings, bursts of energy, experiences are the only realities; according to a fully idealistic interpretation of process philosophy, these terms are names for momentarily developing minds. Whitehead points out:

> A dead nature can give no reasons. All ultimate reasons are in terms of aim at value. A dead nature aims at nothing. It is the essence of life that it exists for its own sake, as the intrinsic reaping of value.
>
> Apart from the experiences of subjects [occasions of experience] there is nothing, nothing, nothing, bare nothingness.

Because of this emphasis on experiences, process philosophy sometimes is called *panexperientialism*.

What we call *things* are really collections of momentarily existing experiences. We are streams of highly complex one-at-a-time experiences that have self-consciousness. Most experiences lack self-consciousness, and vast numbers of this kind of experience, existing many at a time, make up our bodies. However, all experiences, even those that constitute the subatomic particles of a steel beam or a stone, have some feeling, some bit of freedom to select what they enjoy in some rudimentary way. Whitehead maintains that all life has creative activity, aim, and enjoyment. Because all experiences have these, all experiences are alive.

God begins each experience by giving it a tailor-made offer of the perfect plan for it, based on what is possible in the situation at hand. This perfect plan may seem too good to be true, but it is too good not to be true, and deserves full acceptance. Whitehead refers to God as "the lure for feeling" and "the poet of the world, with tender patience leading it by his vision of truth, beauty, and goodness." All past experiences are present in every new experience, though some are far more relevant and in effect more powerful than others. The task of each experience is to choose between the competing influences of God's perfect offer (called *initial aim*—what we often refer to as the indwelling Christ or spark of divinity) and past happenings. Once this choice is made, within a fraction of a second, the experience goes from being a *subject*—a unity of current awareness—to an *object* that no longer experiences, but which God perfectly and permanently keeps and appreciates. All later experiences are in some degree aware of all previous experiences, which are the background in relation to which each new experience chooses in blending influences of the past and the divine possible. The continuing influence of past experiences on later ones in their lines of development is what in New Thought we refer to as the *law of mind* or simply the *law of cause and effect*, or *karma* (which last term generally refers to the influence of events considerably in the past).

The underlying awareness of the feelings of others, of mind within mind, is what is known as *extrasensory perception*. Sensory perception is a more specialized form of the feeling of other feeling. Self-consciousness is a still more complex step in the continuum of awareness, a variation on the same theme. Cosmic (mystical) consciousness is a much fuller, clearer awareness. Since all the past is within every experience, theoretically anyone who concentrates on it sufficiently should be able to know anything by plugging into this remarkable database. This ought not to be surprising to anyone who has come upon the work of Karl Pribram on the universe as holographic or the work of David Bohm on morphic resonance.

Pantheism and Panentheism

This universal arrangement is not *pantheism* (all is God), but *panentheism*, a term devised by Karl C. F. Krause (1781–1832) to describe his thought. It is best known for its use by Charles Hartshorne and recently by Matthew Fox. Panentheism says that all is *in* God, somewhat as if God were the ocean and we were fish. If one considers what is in God's body to be part of God, then we can say that God is all there is and then some. The universe is God's body, but God's awareness or personality is greater than the sum of all the parts of the universe. All the parts have some degree of freedom in cocreating with God. At the start of its momentary career as a subject, an experience is God—as the divine initial aim. As the experience carries on its choosing process, it is a freely aiming reality that is not strictly God, since it departs from God's purpose to some degree. Yet everything is within God.

The most practical value of pantheism is that it recognizes the presence of God everywhere, but it does this at an enormous cost. It provides for the presence of God as the only actor; God's presence is an overriding presence that cancels the possibility of the existence of anything else, of any genuine beloved, of any loving or unloving response to God. In pantheism, human existence or any other finite existence is at best a mystery. Explanation in any satisfying sense is impossible. There can be affirmation that there is nothing but God, but where that leaves the affirmer is unclear; his or her existence is no more than appearance, and enlightenment brings recognition that one's seeming status as a unique, permanent perspective in reality is illusory.

It is not necessary to go to pantheism, with a god that acts as a universal wet blanket, smothering the possibilities of everything else's genuine existence. Panentheism gives all that one could want: an all-encompassing, growing, perfect God, everywhere present and containing everywhere within himself; *and* the reality of oneself and others, freely deciding within God, responding to God's overtures in the process of cocreation. Theism denies that the world (including us) shares in God's being. Panentheism recognizes that everything shares God's being (or becoming) but that God's being operates from innumerable relatively freely choosing centers or perspectives of existence. God and the world, which is God's body, are interdependent. To be is to be free, to be choosing, and to be enjoying (slightly or greatly, positively or negatively) the process of selecting from among competing influences. To be doing this is to be alive. To be doing it with the complexity of performing these tasks self-consciously, rationally,

purposefully is to be doing it as a person. To have perfect awareness of all this, perfect memory, love, and preservation of it, and
to be giving perfect guidance to the others who are involved in
the process is to be the only perfect person, God.

Santiago Sia summarizes Hartshorne's panentheism:

> Panentheism ... holds that God includes the world.
> But it sets itself apart from pantheism in that it does
> not maintain that God and the world are identical. . . .
> Hartshorne explains that God is a whole whose whole-
> properties are distinct from the properties of the con-
> stituents. While this is true of every whole, it is more so
> of God as the supreme whole. . . . The part is distin-
> guishable from the whole although within it. The
> power of the parts is something suffered by the whole,
> not enacted by it. The whole has properties too which
> are not shared by the parts. Similarly, God *as whole* pos-
> sesses attributes which are not shared by his crea-
> tures. . . . We perpetually create content not only in
> ourselves but also in God. And this gives significance to
> our presence in this world.

If we continue to say, as New Thoughters often do, that there
is only one Presence and only one Power, God, the Good omnipotent, we should state it with an awareness of what it means
in a panentheistic perspective. This affirmation may be made
primarily as a recognition that there is no devil, no unified negative cosmic force in opposition to God. When we say that there
is only one Power and Presence, we are saying that the whole
and the part are present in each other. God is present *not* like
a lump of clay or a piece of plastic that can have different shapes
at different times yet remain exactly what it was originally. God is
present as dynamic, loving, alluring divine purpose, as guidance
uniquely offered to each of the innumerably many units of
freely deciding experience. God's power—the attracting power
of perfection—is exercised from within these innumerable centers of choice. In each of these is the dual power of divine offer
and human or nonhuman response, neither of which could op-

erate without the other. This is a contracting or covenanting process. The affirmation that God is working with us—in some sense as us, as the initiator of each experience—can be made much more meaningfully from a panentheistic perspective than from a pantheistic one.

Our linguistic or temperamental preference may determine whether or not we use the term *divine* for the power of response—and the responders (units of responding), including ourselves. For most purposes we refer to God *and* ourselves, for we are free to decide how much we accept of what God offers to us. In mystical moments we emphasize unity, which is the complete or relatively complete acceptance of God's offers. When we consider the divine character of the whole creative process, we are justified in referring to it as only one Power and only one Presence. All unity is a unification of the many, and the many are meaningful only in relation to unity. In Hebrew, the word *achad* means *united one* and is used to refer to God. The alternation of the one and the many is essential to the process of cocreation. *E pluribus unum* (out of many, one) appears on the Great Seal of the United States.

All this cocreating happens so quickly that we are unaware of the separate experiences, which are like the separate frames of a motion picture. Similarly, we are unaware of the separate cells of our bodies, to say nothing of the molecules and atoms that constitute them. We are unaware of most of what is going on within and around us, let alone throughout the universe. We don't need to know the subatomic structure of a kitchen table in order to put groceries onto it, but that doesn't mean that there is no such structure. So it is with the experiential nature of the world. Although we may not be able to focus on the individual frames of our lives, God does; and it is only in relation to them, one by one, that God can give or receive anything. We call this moment-by-moment, cumulative, personal existence *serial selfhood.*

Process New Thought

What we call Process New Thought is New Thought that uses traditional New Thought techniques, but substitutes insights of process philosophy for the traditional substance approaches to philosophy commonly employed in New Thought. In other words, the Process New Thoughter does essentially the same things that the Substance New Thoughter does, but has a different understanding of what is going on. The use of process thought also provides New Thought with new connections to the academic world. Of great importance, a process understanding can cut New Thought's Gordian knot of thinking about the creative process, especially the role of Law in it.

Laws

New Thought places great emphasis on the *lawfulness* of the universe. New Thoughters, like most people, tend to believe that the laws of nature are changeless. However, Whitehead tells us that natural laws are *habits of interaction* of the innumerably many experiences that make up the universe. (Moreover, we can view laws as descriptions or formulations of the habits in question.) He notes that there is no evidence that the laws of nature are changeless, and indeed that

> to judge by all analogy, after a sufficient span of existence our present laws will fade into unimportance. New interests will dominate. In our present sense of the term, our spatio-temporal epoch will pass into the background of the past, which conditions all things dimly and without evident effect . . .

None of this is to say that the habits that we call laws are unreliable; it is just that they probably are not truly permanent. However, the pattern of cocreativity sketched here *is* permanent, since it allows for any changes that eventually might produce different laws. Nor should anything we say about the centrality of experiences as the building blocks of reality suggest unreliability of the great collections of them with which we are familiar. God is still utterly dependable, though the earth be removed and the mountains be carried into the midst of the sea, and substance notions be replaced by process thought.

Apart from the changeableness of laws, there is the more pressing problem of the power of laws. It is understandable that after a few centuries of dramatic scientific discovery of natural laws, people almost worshiped these laws. Most unfortunately, they *reified* laws. *Reification* (from the Latin *res*, thing, and *facere*, to make) is a philosophical term that means to understand a mental entity as if it were a thing. We might call it "thingification." Whitehead referred to it as the "fallacy of misplaced concreteness," mistaking the abstract for the concrete. In this pervasive error, people fail to realize that laws are just descriptions of how reality works, rather than some power that makes things happen. In truth, considering laws as descriptions, *no law ever did anything to or for anyone or anything.* This is not to deny the powerfulness of the states of affairs described, summarized, by laws; those described habits, like our own habits, can be extremely powerful before they are changed.

The Golden Calf of Active Law

Part of New Thought subscribes to the belief that the creative process involves a roundabout, back-and-forth (albeit within God) movement involving an impersonal, automatically responsive side of God called Law, in addition to the side called Love. This alleged Law should not be confused with the general notion of law. Instead, this Law is like a genie or robot, obediently carrying out our commands. In contrast, Quimby's conception of creativity as a direct process of choosing between divine Wisdom and human misconceptions and thereupon directly receiving the result of the choice is consistent with process thought. Quimby's view can be likened to Polaroid photography, in which one chooses the thing to be photographed, presses the shutter release, and the image is developed directly on the film. The later New Thought idea—that one thinks and feels into Law and that Law returns the selected product—is like turning the film over to a photofinisher who processes the film and then returns the pictures. What actually happens is explained later in this chapter in relation to healing.

A scientist or philosopher would say that the photofinisher

view of creativity is not parsimonious, for it introduces an unnecessary middle step into our relationship with God. This violates Occam's Razor or law of parsimony, which says that from rival explanations, one should choose the simplest and most direct.

The notion of active, responsive Law is something like the golden calf that the Children of Israel worshiped, to the chagrin of Moses. Regardless of whether the word *law* is used, there is no adequate reason to believe that there is any such side of God. In Process New Thought, supremely wise Love is seen as all that is needed to explain God's activity in the world.

Why God Cannot Be Law

Why can't there be a responsive God-as-Law, such as many New Thoughters believe in? God does respond in the sense that he gives to *later* experiences initial aims adjusted to the situations produced by the choices of their predecessors. But this response does not shape substance, since there is no enduring substance to shape. Everything is new, moment by moment, however much it may be like what preceded it. We frequently fail to recognize that only the experience of the moment can act. Past experiences continue—without additional action—to be powerful influences, but what they are is fixed forever. Regardless of whether we accept process philosophy, we should realize that we can live only in the moment; process philosophy explains why. We identify ourselves with past and future experiences in our lines of development when we should be concentrating on the question of what God can do for the experience of the moment, for us *right now.* The answer is that all that God can do—and it is plenty—is to give initial aim, the perfect plan for the experience to deal with the situation in which it arises, and to move onward to something at least a little better than the situation in which it arose.

Here are the main considerations against the existence of Law as an impersonal, automatically responsive mental substance:

1. *A commonsense view of reality is inadequate,* particularly the assumption that there is thing-like substance. A thing-like re-

sponsive universal Mind or Law may seem natural, even as God in the form of an old man sitting on a cloud may seem natural. One is as incorrect as the other.

2. *A thingified Law is inconsistent with the known nature of the physical world.* Physicists now know that the physical world is thoroughly processive at bottom. In order to maintain belief in a substantive universal Mind, there would have to be a great dichotomy between the natures of God and the world, a dichotomy that would prevent an overall unity. There would be a house of totality divided against itself.

3. *God is supremely good.* God wants the very best for every experience, not just for its successors. An experience chooses and enjoys for only a fraction of a second. This choosing is a response to what God already has done for it in giving it the very best plan that could be offered. Whatever is given to an experience must be given to it at the start of its moment of developing. God could do nothing greater for it, even if God under the curious name of Law were able to respond to it during its extremely brief career. An experience experiences only once, and it must be in that moment that it receives and gives.

4. *Each experience is isolated.* Although an experience contains all of the past, once an experience is started on its way of momentary development, it receives no more input. When it has finished its rapid cocreation, it itself becomes its gift to later experiences, even as all earlier experiences were gifts to it. (If it seems strange that an experience knows only the past and not what currently is developing around it, consider that all well-educated people know that physically we receive only information coming from the past: light emitted by stars centuries ago, from our sun about eight minutes ago, sounds produced perhaps a second ago, the pain of being struck by an object a fraction of a second before the message reaches the brain.) What God does not do by acting within the experience as its alluring initial aim God can never do for that experience.

5. *The supposed Law lacks freedom* in having to respond mechanically, "mathematically" to what is fed into it. That is inconsistent with freedom in all experiences, including the divine experience, and there are only experiences.

6. *God can't give a completed product.* Those who believe in Law hold that Law gives people completed products, material or non-material. Process thought maintains that the only gifts that God can give to an experience (in addition to the harmonious arrangement of the past in the Divine Mind) is the experience's initial aim. God cannot give a completed product, such as believers in Law envision.

7. *Finite entities aren't able to come up with perfect plans.* We usually assume that it is up to us to discover what possibilities are open to us and to select from them. We seldom consider what a monumental task this is, since the possibilities are endless. If it is difficult for human beings, what must it be for animals lacking self-consciousness, to say nothing of lower levels of reality? We may speak of the instincts of animals, but we seldom attempt to say exactly what instinct is. Process philosophy recognizes that nothing less than infinite, loving, willing, personal Intelligence is adequate to do the job of selecting from among the infinite possibilities for realization, and this philosophy maintains that God offers the perfect plan to each experience. It is God who makes possible the departure from the pattern of the past; in other words, without God there could be no newness, only endless repetition, if even that were possible, which it is not, since all creation is cocreation with God.

8. *Only personal Love-Wisdom is all-sufficient, not the implied mechanistic materialism of the impersonal Ultimate.* When Law is conceived as an impersonal yet intelligent responsive reality, it is asked to perform a function that only the supremely personal is adequate to exercise. Leading, luring, orchestrating the universe (of however many dimensions, planes, or whatever there may be) is a job that only the perfectly personal Reality can do. Belief in an Ultimate that is even partly impersonal in essence (as distinguished from the many impersonal parts of God's all-inclusive body) is hardly different from belief in materialism. To resort to the belief that Divine Mind (as distinguished from God's body, the universe) is in any degree impersonal, or that the ultimately personal is in any degree unreliable or lacking in impartiality, is simply to fail to understand how gloriously ade-

quate the personal God of love-intelligence is to guide every experience throughout the universe.

As Emmet Fox used to say, the Lord is my shepherd, not my bellhop.

Don't Ride the Epicycles

Any of our conclusions about what God and the world are like should be tentative, but some of us believe that the process interpretation of New Thought is a much closer approximation of the truth than is the old substance interpretation. The notion of an active, responsive, impersonal Law is as antiquated and needless as the old theories of phlogiston to explain combustion, or epicycles (circles within circles) to explain the paths of heavenly bodies assumed to be moving around an immobile Earth at the center of the universe. Such theories did provide a helpful orderliness to the universe for anyone who believed them, but one can scarcely imagine resorting to them after encountering more adequate explanations.

Demythologize or Die, at Least Intellectually

Belief in a fully personal (self-conscious, rational, purposeful) God of unimaginably wondrously wise love, initiating—but never compelling—all that goes on, may be challenging, but it is the best explanation that anyone has offered yet for how the universe works. Nevertheless, the old view of an impersonal active Law can continue to be a useful myth for those who find it helpful, who have no taste for demythologizing, and who are too set in their ways to change. We hope that Process New Thought will come naturally to people who are new to New Thought and carry with them few, if any, substance assumptions. It is not so much that people who are firmly committed to theories change their minds as it is that progress is made funeral by funeral, as quantum discoverer Max Planck observed about science.

A Doctrinal Updating Through the Open Top

Although an emphasis on supposedly active, responsive Law is not limited to any one New Thought group, it may be most notably found in Religious Science. The famous Holmes "What I [now "We"] Believe" statement, presented in chapter 2, requires only minimal change to be compatible with both substance and process understandings. "We believe that God is personal to all who feel this Indwelling Presence" could become *We believe that God is personal and is experienced as such by all who feel this Indwelling Presence.* "We believe that the Universal Spirit, which is God, operates though a Universal Mind, which is the Law of God; and that we are surrounded by this Creative Mind which receives the direct impress of our thought and acts upon it" could become *We believe that the Universal Spirit, the Creative Mind, which is God, operates in a completely impartial and orderly way and, through cocreation with us, brings about results in exact proportion to the degree that we accept the perfection offered by God.* It also would be helpful to substitute *everlasting* for "eternal" in the statement of belief, in order to avoid the problem of which definition of "eternal" is intended. Holmes's comment that Religious Science is "open at the top" allows for such updating.

A perennial task of religions and philosophies for living is to express themselves in terms that are most understandable and acceptable in the times and places in which they operate. In order to spread its gospel throughout the ancient Mediterranean world, Christianity had to speak in terms of Greek philosophy. It selected the philosophy of Plato and remained with it until switching to the philosophy of Aristotle in the Middle Ages; later, leaders of the Protestant Reformation largely turned back to Plato. Now various philosophies, including process philosophy, compete in conceptualizing the essence of Christianity. In some respects, process philosophy, which has made progress in both Protestant and Catholic circles, is an updating of Plato.

Similarly, Holmes and the other pioneers of New Thought faced the task of explaining the *fact* of spiritual healing by some *theory.* Understandably, they used forms of metaphysics then available to them. At the time, opting for a substantialist, emanationist, impersonalist outlook may have been justified in order to break free from the notion of an anthropomorphic God, but that old substance metaphysics certainly no longer can be taken for granted.

Our greatest tribute to the founders of New Thought is to use their efforts as helps on the way to greater understanding and use of divine gifts than any of us has yet achieved. New Thought began in bodily healing, and it is appropriate to express the most significant new understanding of New Thought in relation to the movement's original and continuing concern with healing.

Healing

A process understanding of reality has great implications in relation to healing. The cumulative nature of experience is vital to understanding healing of any sort. The current past cannot be changed, but moment by moment the past grows larger. It is modified by the character of each new experience that becomes part of the past. To the extent that we make ourselves more rather than less like what God offers to us, we enrich the positive nature of the past. In this way, we reduce the contrast between the past and the initial aims offered by God in the future. This reduction of contrast is what we do in any treatment, whether by prayer, surgery, medicine, or whatever. The less the contrast between past and perfect, the easier it is for upcoming experiences to accept the perfect, and the perfect always is healing—whole-making—in some sense. This is why we can promote the healing of others by healing our own consciousness in recognizing them as perfect expressions of God. Conversely, negative thinking, contrary to God's offers, increases the contrast between past and perfect and makes acceptance of God's offers proportionately more difficult, although never impossible.

Other Advantages of Process New Thought

In addition to this new understanding of healing, Process New Thought has numerous other advantages; eighteen are given in

Alan's *A Guide to the Selection and Care of Your Personal God.* Here we shall restrain ourselves and mention only a few. Primarily, there is a tremendous freeing psychological power that you get when you realize that you are new every moment in God's love, as a song written by Deb puts it. You didn't make all those errors of the past; your ancestors did it! You exist for only a moment, and you can afford to go completely with God and risk all for the greatest divine reward of fully accepting God as your life. None of your efforts ever is lost; each one is preserved in full clarity forever in God and helps to shape all of reality forevermore.

Recapitulation

Now it should be clear why the *divine* job description provides for God to *start everything,* to *finish nothing,* and to *keep everything,* while *your* job description calls for you to *start nothing,* to *finish very quickly* what God starts for you, and to realize that *you can't keep anything* for more than a moment.

Reconceptualizing New Thought in process terms includes the substitution of *impartial* for *impersonal* and *constant* for *changeless* in speaking of God, and abandoning Law in favor of the all-sufficiency of divine Love. We are left totally, thrillingly, dancingly dependent on the completely reliable, persistent, dynamic ultimate Love that offers only the best to everyone and everything. This Love forever cherishes the completed experiences from all visible and invisible dimensions of the universe. God inspires and lovingly preserves everything. Each freely choosing burst of life produces a unique perspective that forever enriches the always-growing God.

Below we have summed up the co-creative process (all creation is, and always has been, co-creation) of continuing, ever-new divine contracting or covenanting in a formula. We have thrown in a table of some major differences between conventional Christianity and substance and process versions of New Thought. Then, in the next chapter, recognizing that very few subatomic particles in steel beams will decide to enjoy themselves by reading this book, we shall turn our attention from a discussion of the subatomic structure of everything, including the kitchen table, to the highly complex experiences who are more interested in unpacking the groceries and starting to fix dinner.

Creativity Formula

Past + Divine Offer + Choice = Co-Creation

TABLE 3

SOME CONTRASTS OF OLD AND NEW OUTLOOKS
Adapted from C. Alan Anderson, *Healing Hypotheses*

Old Christian Thought	Substance New Thought	Process New Thought
Reality is enduring substance.	Reality is enduring substance.	Reality is creative process.
Being is basic.	Being is basic.	Becoming is basic.
You *have* experience.	You *have* experience.	You *are* experience.
Soul is mortal substance.	Soul is immortal substance.	Soul is a succession of momentarily existing selves (serial selfhood).
Resurrection.	Subjective immortality.	Objective and subjective immortality.
God is largely transcendent (classical theism).	God is essentially immanent (pantheism).	God is immanent and transcendent (panentheism).
God creates out of nothing *(ex nihilo)*.	God emanates from divine fulness.	God co-creates by participating in blending of past and possible.
God created the universe.	God created the universe.	God always has had a universe of some sort; all creation is co-creation; this always has been so.
Universe is not part of God; it is matter and mind created by God.	Universe is part (in some interpretations, all) of God's being, is God's body.	Universe is part of God's becoming, is God's body.

Matter is lifeless stuff created by God.	Matter is appearance of one mind (God).	Matter is collection of many relatively lowly minds (experiences)
God is changeless in theory, if not in practice.	God is changeless, except as responsive.	God is growing experientially, yet constant morally.
God is love, yet is forcing.	God is Love-Law.	God is wise, alluring, persuasive Love.
God is personal and perhaps somewhat arbitrary.	God is partly impersonal, and acts as Law.	God is personal, impartial, and acts by giving initial aims.
God gives orders.	God gives general possibilities.	God gives tailor-made possibilities (initial aims).
God creates and sustains, yet often seems inactive in one's life.	The burden of initiation in creation in our lives is on us. God guides and responds.	God initiates. We must respond to God's guiding initiation of each moment.
Prayer sometimes changes God, who may give what is requested.	Prayer changes us. We receive according to our beliefs, working through divine Law shaping unformed substance.	Prayer (a form of acceptance of God's offerings) helps create momentary self, giving immediate enjoyment and enriching the next self's past by becoming part of it, thereby making it easier for the next self to accept God's initial aim.
Christ is identified solely with Jesus.	Christ is the presence of God permanently in each of us equally.	Christ is the presence of God, understood as initial aim of each momentary self (occasion of experience).
Law is divine command.	Law is active, divine, impersonal, automatic, intelligent, unconscious part of God.	Law is an abstraction describing habits of interaction of occasions of experience.

7

*

Growing Practical Application of New Thought

Critics and Corrections

New Thought has always had its share of detractors. These critics either are materialists who do not believe in the power of the mind to influence the body, or they have tried to force their outcomes with sheer will power; or they have failed to persevere in their efforts, like the people who diet every afternoon between lunch and dinner. Many of these critics have proved the power of the mind very effectively by thinking negative thoughts and getting negative outcomes. Like attracts like!

Some critics are basically unfamiliar with what New Thought is about. They think that it involves empty platitudes or whistling past the graveyard, and is out of touch with reality. Other critics confuse New Thought with New Age, thinking that it is somehow significantly involved with the occult. Still other critics are members of traditional religions who believe that a religion should not be based on what is easy or what works, but on what is "true," as if what works or what is easy could not possibly be true. Such critics frequently feel that their religion is somehow threatened or weakened by removing its gloom and negativity. They expect life to be nasty, brutish, and short, so for them it is. They have their reward, as Jesus said of the Pharisees.

A critic who may belong to this latter group is Richard Huber, author of *The American Idea of Success*. Huber studied American success literature from Benjamin Franklin through 1973, when his book was published. Success literature after Franklin and his nineteenth-century successors is almost entirely based on New Thought principles, whether or not it is identified as such. Huber's criticism, therefore, is implicitly of New Thought, and in several chapters he zeros in on it overtly. Success, he states, used to be based on belief that it meant that God approves of you, and that the rich should give to the church, which would in turn give to the poor. Perish the thought that some upstart philosophy of healthy-mindedness should teach the poor to stop being poor and eliminate the middle man; why, the church might lose some of its power base! And these New Thought ministers have the audacity to take the research of serious scholars and simplify or paraphrase it to make it available to their congregations. Huber seems offended by the notion that anyone anywhere might actually be enjoying life, or expecting financial prosperity, or even anything pleasant to happen.

Huber describes the success literature and New Thought mostly accurately, but his tone is snide, as if to dig the reader in the ribs and say, "We know better than this, don't we?" His discovery was that in the past fifty years (thirty at the time he wrote), something has been missing from success literature that was there before, especially in the writings of Franklin. That something is the *character ethic.*

Huber points out that writers such as Dale Carnegie (*How to Win Friends and Influence People*) concentrated on what he calls the *personality ethic,* making oneself pleasing and influential to others. Character, on the other hand, involves qualities such as integrity, fairness, loyalty, honesty, perseverance, and service to others. Says Huber, "The new market for success literature . . . lacked hardness of mind and toughness of character," and he compares the success idea to "a toasted marshmallow—a lovely golden brown on the outside, but soft and mushy at the center." However, he admits—in tiny print in an endnote—that Napoleon Hill, who laid enormous stress on character in his writings, based on his twenty-year study of successful people, is an exception. He grants that Orison Swett Marden was highly successful in the hotel business, and more than once managed to rise from the ashes of defeat, but to Huber that is unremarkable. Also, he seems to have overlooked the extensive New Thought literature that interprets the Bible symbolically and emphasizes the strong character development of various biblical figures. But perhaps his biggest *gaffe* was taking seriously Charles Fillmore's parody of the Twenty-third Psalm, which begins, "The Lord is my banker; my credit is good."

Despite Huber's numerous cheap shots, his basic premise is valid: there is a noticeable lack of emphasis on developing good character, not just in much of our current success literature, but in our society as a whole. Public schools are forbidden to teach such character builders as the Ten Commandments, children are taught to esteem themselves complacently even when they are behaving irresponsibly and incompetently, and the discipline of spirituality is never discussed. But Huber offers no remedy for those whose needs are not being met in the traditional main-stream churches or those who have no religion. He expresses no appreciation for those who offer hope and the oil of the personality ethic for the wheels of social interactions, communi-cation skills that are frequently essential for success. Perhaps there never was a good idea that someone didn't come along and take too far. Certainly, it is possible to misuse and abuse the power of the mind, to pick up the *new* and the *positive* parts while overlooking the *thought* and the *thinking* parts.

The founders of New Thought all postulated good character; they simply took it for granted. The 1904 Constitution of the New Thought Federation (a forerunner of the INTA) included the phrase "health, happiness, and character." Napoleon Hill's emphasis on character came from his own upbringing and from the successful people whom he interviewed over twenty years. And Emmet Fox used to say, "You have to have your *wish*bone backed up with a *back*bone." References to the importance of the character ethic are frequently found in New Thought litera-ture. But the writers didn't dwell on character or single it out for special attention. The emphasis in New Thought has been on the freedom that it offers those who have felt oppressed by some traditional religions and on undoing some of the damage that negative, limited thinking has done in people's lives. In the process of showing pity to victims, it may at times have neglected to emphasize the importance of strong character as the principal means of taking control of one's life and ending victimhood once and for all. The discipline required to make New Thought work is an aspect of character. Certainly, mystical alignment with God must constitute the supreme aspect of high character.

Recovering the Missing Ingredient

Happily, another writer has made a study of the success literature and noted the absence of emphasis on the character ethic. Unlike Huber, he offers a simple remedy: put it back. He outlines the importance of a "principle-centered, character-based, inside-out approach to life" in his blockbuster best-seller, *The Seven Habits of Highly Effective People*. He is Stephen Covey, and like Huber, he comes from outside the New Thought movement. His book is growing increasingly popular in New Thought, where it is beginning to be used for study groups; it is listed as available through *Science of Mind* magazine.

The Seven Habits deal with walking the spiritual path. They help us to go from dependence to independence:

> Be proactive.
> Begin with the end in mind.
> Put first things first.

then to interdependence, with each other and with God:

> Think win/win.
> Seek first to understand, then to be understood.
> Synergize.

The seventh habit, *Sharpen the saw*, refers to balance in our lives, to maintaining both our production and our production capability, or as Covey puts it, to giving attention both to the golden eggs and to the goose that lays them.

These habits teach us how to plan our daily lives around our goals and our life's mission, and to use our beliefs and goals as a basis for making decisions. Because Covey is a highly successful business consultant, his book is generally kept in the business section of bookstores, where people hunting for books on spirituality would not ordinarily look. Yet Covey uses examples from his relationships with his wife and children, as well as from business, to illustrate his points; and he clearly has deep spiritual convictions of his own, even though he may not consider himself a New Thoughter.

Restoring the emphasis on character to New Thought results in an explosion of power. Building on the personality ethic is like building on sand. Building on character is like building on rock. As we have already mentioned, developing a pleasing personality and good communication skills are important and necessary, but character must come first. Character plus personality plus an understanding of the power of mind, with a belief in one Presence and Power that is good and with which we are all one, equals spiritual TNT that moves mountains.

Self-Discipline, Mastery, and Freedom

Another contemporary author outside of New Thought who offers insight into the character weakness of the American people and the self-discipline implicit in the character ethic for those on a spiritual path is George Leonard. In his book *Mastery,* Leonard defines mastery as working at something for its own sake, "the mysterious process during which what is at first difficult becomes progressively easier and more pleasurable through practice." He illustrates it with examples from sports, especially from his favorite martial art, aikido (he runs an aikido school), but states that it applies to all learning. He points out that our quick-fix, instant gratification, consumerist society is at war with the mastery principle, that it has eroded our value system with models such as the TV commercial in which people work for one and a half seconds and then it's Miller Time.

In mastery, we frequently reach a plateau where we are making no apparent progress, but "the most important learning and development takes place during your time on the plateau." It has been said that success is a journey, not a destination. Mastery also involves the journey rather than the destination, practice for the sake of practice, and learning to love the plateau. Our life's mission is more of a journey than a destination, and changing our thought—ruling our mind—certainly involves mastery. "What's in it for me" is the intrinsic reward of mastery rather than some extrinsic reward such as money or fame.

Implicit in the mastery concept is full attention to the present moment, which is necessary to get into the flow of what one is doing. Since we can live only one moment at a time, it is unfortunate to waste it by attending exclusively to the past or the future. Yet this is what so many of us do so much of the time, in a state of preoccupation that prevents mastery because we just aren't there mentally; we're somewhere else. A great researcher with a name that sounds like a sneeze, Csikszentmihalyi, has written a book titled *Flow* (by the time they got his name on the cover, that was all there was room for). His research over many years showed that people are happiest when their work allows them to get into a state of flow in which they are fully engrossed in what they are doing in the present moment.

Strong character in general, and mastery in particular, are both related to self-discipline. Say "discipline" and most people wince. It brings back memories of childhood punishment or distasteful school activities. One of us (Deb) had a graduate school professor who used to give a workshop on discipline for teachers. Participants formed two concentric circles which then paired up with each other, one of each pair being "teacher" and the other, "student." Opening lines of a script were supplied; for example: Teacher says, "Who threw that Twinkie?" and Student replies, "Nobody; it took off all by itself!" Participants continued to role-play, improvising the rest of the script. Then the roles were reversed, and with new opening statements each participant got to experience the opposite role. In debriefing afterward, participants were amazed to learn that everyone preferred the role of student, despite all the old fears associated with discipline. The student has the freedom and creativity, not the person attempting to impose discipline on another. Discipline is best when self-imposed as a means to a self-chosen end. Disciplining one's thoughts is essential to New Thought.

Expert dog handlers agree that a dog who has had good obedience training is happier and more contented. This is because such a dog can *do* more, has more skills, is more competent than a dog left to its own devices. Paradoxical though it may seem, the disciplined dog has more freedom, in part because it is more trustworthy, both to itself and to its owner.

Freedom is a basic need for all living creatures, one of the needs encoded in our genes because it has survival value. But simply opening the cage is not true freedom if the creature lacks the skills to survive. Animal mothers patiently drill their babies in necessary survival skills before turning them loose in the wild. Similarly, religions bind (*re ligio*) their adherents into various disciplines with the intention of giving them skills for coping with life and for growing spiritually. But for many people these spiritual disciplines fail, either because they have been imposed from without or because they do not meet individual needs. Such people struggle to break free. Once out of the cage, they still lack spiritual survival skills; they are undisciplined. It's as if they were to live on a diet of nothing but hot fudge sundaes with no exercise, and then discover themselves running in the Boston Marathon.

The price of freedom may well be eternal vigilance, but the royal road to freedom is the route of self-discipline, the mastery described by Leonard and taught by Covey. It consists of first getting very clear on what your mission in life is, choosing your goals based on that mission, and then doing whatever it takes to reach them. There is no external coercion, no loss of freedom to choose, only the gaining of what you truly want, be that health, wealth, happiness, or all of the above. You have or can obtain all the resources you need to reach any goals that you decide to set, because you are one with the one Presence and Power in the universe, and that Power is good.

The path to freedom is to do what you love. *Do What You Love, the Money Will Follow,* is *Science of Mind* columnist Marsha Sinetar's title for the best known of her books. New Thought is about love, not about greed. There is no need to be greedy in an abundant universe. Greed comes from a belief in lack and limitation. But by voluntarily limiting or narrowing yourself down from a universe of choices to just the choices that carry you toward your chosen goal, you gain that goal, and with it, the satisfaction of having what you really want. This is what Jesus meant when he said, "Strait is the gate, and narrow is the way, which leadeth unto life" (Matt. 7:14).

The character building and mastery in New Thought are freely chosen. No one and no institution imposes them on us. No sense of duty compels us, no shame inhibits us, no fear of punishment drives us. We are following our own God-given perfect possibilities, our own deepest and truest desires; and by joyfully becoming the most we can be, we glorify God.

Character has little or nothing to do with keeping to the letter of the law. Jesus did not hesitate to break religious laws when they interfered with human needs, as when he and his followers "harvested on the Sabbath" by breaking off ears of corn in the field and eating them. And he regularly lambasted the Pharisees for their hypocrisy in adhering to the letter of the Law ad absurdum: "Ye tithe mint and rue" (Luke 11:42) while failing to keep to the spirit of the Law. He also berated them for making up laws of their own and passing them off as the will of God, paraphrasing the Old Testament words of God to make his point: "But in vain do they worship me, teaching for doctrines the commandments of men" (Matt. 15:9 and Mark 7:7). God isn't going to "get" us if we miss the mark, but we need to obey the spirit of the Law—the traditional teachings—rather than the letter. At the same time, it is true that the universe is lawful (a different sense of the word *law*) because God is utterly dependable. As Christian apologist C. S. Lewis has pointed out, God uses natural laws to provide a neutral environment so that we can exercise our free will. God is not going to change those laws to benefit anybody or even any group of bodies. Even if the Pope and Billy Graham jump off the Empire State Building holding hands and praying all the way down, God won't turn off the law of gravity, and they will go splat on the sidewalk (an admittedly unlikely scenario). Hence, we are punished *by* our sins, not *for* them. And we still have a lot to learn about how the universe operates.

Many experts on comparative religion have pointed out principles such as the Golden Rule that are found through time and across cultures in nearly every religion. These are the principles Covey alludes to. There is also "the Father within," the inner knowing of the mystic, who experiences God directly. It is the Father within that we turn to as "our refuge and strength, a very present help in trouble" (Ps. 46), for "in Thy presence is the fullness of joy." Ernest Holmes said, "God *in* us, *as* us, *is* us." We can rely on a Power greater than our own, yet at the same time we are part of that Power and share in its glory, as a drop of ocean water shares all the characteristics of the ocean. By becoming still and centered, we contact that Power and align ourselves with it. This takes discipline and practice. Guided by the Father within, we find ourselves persistently acting fairly and honestly, serving, and above all, loving. This is the character ethic.

Creeping into the Culture

Whether or not recent New Thought literature has emphasized the development of character, New Thought—albeit unrecognized as such—has crept into our culture to a remarkable degree. The influence of mainstream ministers Peale and Schuller accounts for much of it, as do the writings of Emmet Fox and Napoleon Hill. People nearly everywhere feel that they must at least give lip service to the importance of having a positive outlook. A study by Matlin and Stang (*The Pollyanna Principle*) some years ago revealed that most people feel that they are a bit above average in most ways: looks, health, prosperity. This means that the average person is a bit above average, like the children in Lake Wobegon!

However, it's what you believe deep down that counts, not what you give lip service to, and you tend to get what you truly expect. Many people just going through the motions of positive thinking fail to set goals or to assess their current actuality. They take off with no compass and no flight plan, then they crash and burn. This reinforces the cynics in their belief that positive thinking is bunk. But as one British wit said of Christianity, it hasn't failed, it just hasn't been tried!

Schuller attempted to correct people's misinterpretations of what Peale was saying by calling his own positive philosophy "possibility thinking" (now "power thinking") and emphasizing the need to "Put a beam under your dream," "Problems are guidelines, not stop signs," and "Tough times never last, but tough people do." He warned people to expect naysayers and discouragement. Emmet Fox, too, attempted to avoid the quick-fix mentality, saying that when you come to church, you shouldn't check your common sense with your hat at the door. The keys to New Thought are mental discipline coupled with positive expectancy, in the context of spiritually uplifted consciousness attuned to God as one's wholly adequate resource. With those in place, even seemingly impossible promises of good can come true, and it may sometimes be easy (unless, of course, you believe it's going to be hard!).

Change Your Thinking for the Gipper

One of the most recent non–New Thought positive thinkers to come onto the success playing field is Tom Morris, a Southern Baptist professor at a Roman Catholic university, whose most remarkable achievement to date is making philosophers out of the Notre Dame football team. Morris, in his book titled *True Success: A New Philosophy of Excellence,* makes clear that he has read Covey and includes character in his list of seven Cs of Success, which he sails at the reader in seven chapters:

1. A Conception of What We Want
2. A Confidence to See Us Through
3. A Concentration on What It Takes
4. A Consistency in What We Do
5. A Commitment of Emotion
6. A Character of High Quality
7. A Capacity to Enjoy

Morris does an exemplary job of zeroing in on the fine distinctions that make generalities work. For example, he points out that there are only three possible causes for inconsistent, self-defeating behaviors: ignorance, indifference, and inertia. "This is a complete basic diagnosis of the psychology of inconsistency. Ignorance is a matter of the mind. Indifference is a matter of the heart. Inertia is a matter of the will." He goes on to explain that the cure for ignorance is information, and the cure for indifference and inertia is the imagination. (And abundant alliteration!)

A Digression About Depression

This may be a good place to discuss the difference between thinking behaviors and feeling behaviors, customarily called emotions. We aren't born emotional, even if we're Italian. Emotions are collections of sensations from our bodies and the world outside. They are learned behaviors, part of the brain's attempts to make sense out of the sensory input from the outside world. According to William Glasser; building on the work of William Powers (two Bills: a paradox, that's two doctors), we are constantly comparing what we have (the input from the outside world) with what we want (the model of the world as we would like it to be that we build in our minds). When what we have turns out to be exactly what we want, we experience pure feeling, in this case, pleasure. It lasts only a few minutes, and its message is, "Great! Don't change a thing!" When what we have is not what we want, we experience some amount of pure pain. It also lasts only a few minutes, and its message is "Do something different, dummy!" Our response to that pain message is to *behave* in some way: to think, act, or feel. We might, for example, choose a depressing behavior in an effort to elicit sympathy. These choices of behavior are, as we have said, usually unconscious.

If we change our behavior and get what we want, painful feeling is replaced by pure pleasure, at least for a few minutes. Emotions are feeling behaviors, which are chosen. The easiest and quickest way to change your emotions is to change your thinking, i.e., choose a different behavior. That's why it's called New Thought, not New Emotion. The catch is that having undesirable behaviors, in this case, emotions, gets to be a habit. Replacing bad habits is where mastery and self-discipline come in.

Meanwhile, back in South Bend, Tom Morris explains,

There are people whose artificially energetic, chirpy cheerfulness is over the top and alienates as many people as it attracts. You don't need to be *always* singing, whistling, or talking in a loud, fast-paced, and jolly voice about all the wonderful aspects of the day, the job, or the people around you. But you can clearly communicate positive emotion and care by your positive demeanor. Pleasantness is certainly better than grumpiness.

Morris does not quote Emerson, "Nothing great was ever achieved without enthusiasm." But he could have. He does walk us through a philosopher's examination of what success is—and isn't. He stresses the importance of making sure that the values behind our goals are directly related to the goals themselves, and he explains the difference between desires and goals (commitment).

Morris makes it clear that he is talking about the importance of spiritual health for success, about spirituality, not religiosity. Yet implicit in what he is saying is the idea of a friendly universe in which we are free to pursue success and happiness. Like Covey's Seven Habits, True Success works wonderfully well in combination with New Thought. And like New Thought, neither author attempts to prescribe specific religious practices beyond believing in the friendliness of the universe.

It's Not Just for Sunday Any More

Our religion or our philosophy—our belief system—should be synonymous with our way of life. It should be something that we think about and act on seven days a week. It should make life easier, richer, and more satisfying, not difficult and sterile. It should help us to find answers and solutions, to get needs of all kinds met. It should put shoes on the baby, new clothes on Dad, Mom through law school, and allow the whole family to take a vacation instead of developing ulcers and hypertension. It should encourage us to get up again when we're down, and impel us to thankfulness when we're riding high and the world is our oyster. Come to think of it, it should supply the little fork and the cocktail sauce, too.

8

✳

New Thought in Practice

*I*t's one thing to read about New Thought and agree intellectually that a positive attitude is a good idea; it's quite another matter to assimilate it so that you put it into practice automatically when life hands out lemons.

Robert Schuller is fond of pointing out that over 93 percent of the input we receive daily from radio, television, newspapers, and conversation from each other is negative. Small wonder we have a hard time being positive! It takes commitment and determination and effort to change the percentages. At the same time, it does no good simply to resist the idea of negativity, to fight evil, because what you resist persists. Jesus said, "Resist not evil" (Matt. 5:39), and went on to speak of turning the other cheek, which means to look at the other side of the situation. St. Paul added, "Be not overcome of evil, but overcome evil with good" (Rom. 12:21). All of this means looking for opportunities to pile up the positive, to notice the good that exists everywhere, to put your attention on the solution instead of the problem. But we have to keep at it consistently, or we slide right back down the slippery slope under the weight of all that negative input. *Change Your Mind—and Keep the Change* is the title of a book by two NLP teacher-practitioners, Steve and Connirae Andreas.

New Thought likes to borrow from the seventeenth-century mystic Brother Lawrence and talk about "the practice of the presence of God," to which we add "for practical purposes." Brother Lawrence felt God's presence even as he scoured the pots and pans in the monastery kitchen. He fulfilled what he believed was his mission in life and was happy. More precisely, he made himself happy by the way he chose to think. We can apply our newer understanding to our lives and missions just as he did, and we, too, will be happy.

Support for New Thought from Psychology

New Thought in practice begins with what you give your attention to. Research in psychology supports the adage that what you give your attention to grows. *Attention* by definition is "activities relating to the taking in of information from some particular aspect of the environment." Our perceptual systems are set to take in information about what we are interested in. All of us know this to be true when we stop and think about it. A simple example: you become interested in a certain make and style of car, and suddenly you see it everywhere. New Thoughters like to say, "Thoughts held in mind produce after their kind," or "Like attracts like," or "As in heaven (mind), so on earth (manifestation)." They love to tell stories such as Unity minister Mary Katherine MacDougall's account of the lady who loved flowers but had recently moved to an apartment where she could no longer have a garden. She began to think about flowers constantly, to borrow library books about flowers, and to go to flower shows. A few weeks later, for her birthday, without her saying a word about it, three friends sent fresh flowers, two sent bulbs, one sent a window box of plants, and there were flowers by her plate when she was taken out to dinner.

If that sounds too much like ordinary coincidence, consider the new evidence from quantum physics that subatomic particles that make up the universe are somehow linked, and affecting one can affect another, no matter how great the distance between them. Or consider the true story of the scientist with a random event generator, a machine that he used to turn a heat lamp on and off at random in order to warm an outbuilding on his property. Funny thing was, he found that it wasn't working randomly: it was on more than it was off. Investigation revealed that his cat had been sneaking into the shed. Now cats, sybaritic creatures that they are, love warmth. So the cat obviously . . .

hmmm! If the mind of a cat can turn a heat lamp on just because it wants to, what might a human being accomplish?

The bad news is that all too often we use this focused attention principle in reverse. We think about ill health and we get it. We dwell on lack and limitation and we lose our job or our pay is cut. (When a lot of us do this at the same time, it's called a recession.) We rehearse our partner's shortcomings—silently or aloud—and they intensify. And this doesn't seem hard to believe at all: we *know* that it works. But when New Thought comes along and suggests that we are all part of a good God giving us perfect possibilities in an abundant universe, it may seem too good to be true!

Closely linked to attention is *expectancy,* about which psychologists have done huge amounts of research. The best-known name in this field is Julian Rotter, whose expectancy theory states that we generally tend to get what we expect. We set up self-fulfilling prophecies, and then we are surprised when they come true. What happens is that we unconsciously send out subtle cues to the universe, telling it how to treat us. Brain research on neuronal networks shows how negative—or positive—thoughts proliferate. Like attracts like.

Among the newest psychological research with bearing on New Thought in practice is the research on *learned optimism* by Martin Seligman, who has written a book with that title. Seligman first spent many years of research on helplessness and discovered that helplessness is learned and can be *un*learned. Then he expanded his research to optimism and pessimism and discovered that they, too, are learned. They're related to expectancy and to one's explanatory style. We explain things in terms of how personal, pervasive, and persistent they are (Seligman, like Morris, adores alliteration). *Personal* means how much we do or don't affect the outcome of an event. *Pervasive* means how much of life it involves, and *persistent* means whether or not it lasts. A pessimist explains an event with a negative outcome as "all my fault," "messing up my entire life," and "it'll always be this way." An optimist does the opposite. On the other hand, an optimist explains an event with a positive outcome by taking credit personally for it, looking for far-reaching benefits to result, and expecting good fortune to continue. A pessimist was "just lucky," knows it won't amount to much, and is sure it can't last.

Numerous studies showed that pessimists are far more in touch with reality (philosophers call it *actuality*) than optimists, *but* optimists *do* better, far better than pessimists, on any measure you care to name. Mild pessimism does have its uses at certain times. But *habitual* pessimism just gets us what we expect. Habitual optimists, on the other hand, are healthier, live longer while suffering fewer age-related ailments, get better grades in school, and are more likely to get elected to public office than their more pessimistic colleagues. Optimists perform better on the job, are more persevering, and are less likely to get depressed than are pessimists.

In the seminar that we give called The Love Process, Deb describes in detail the techniques that Seligman uses to change habitual pessimists into habitual optimists. One of them is the technique used by Quimby and by Myrtle Fillmore: disputation. So none of this is new to New Thought. But Seligman does have a few refinements for us. He says,

> Learned optimism is not a rediscovery of the "power of positive thinking." The skills of optimism do not emerge from the pink Sunday-school world of happy events. They do not consist in learning to say positive things to yourself. We have found over the years that positive statements you make to yourself have little if any effect. What *is* crucial is what you think when you fail, using the power of "non-negative thinking." Changing the destructive things you say to yourself when you experience the setbacks that life deals all of us is the central skill of optimism.

We might add here that positive statements are valuable as blueprints of what you want, but if you stop and think about it, what is the deep-down belief of the person who goes around affirming "I am prosperous, I am prosperous"? Obviously, the person doesn't *feel* prosperous, or he or she wouldn't have to repeat it over and over. Do you go around affirming "The sun will rise in the east tomorrow"? What Seligman is referring to here is mindless repetition rather than desire backed by patience, a plan, and follow-through with the expectation of eventual success. It's rather like the definition someone once gave for confidence: "going after Moby Dick with a harpoon in one hand and a jar of tartar sauce in the other."

New Thought has always been optimistic, believing as it does in one Presence and one Power, which is good. Now science has come up with support for such beliefs.

Our beliefs create our experiences, and not the other way around, as most people think. The research on optimism is one demonstration of this. Tony Robbins, a popular motivational speaker and author of *Awaken the Giant Within*, explains that our beliefs are like tabletops, and we go around searching for legs—evidence—to support these beliefs. Our evidence—the legs for our tabletop beliefs—may be thin and spindly or thick and massive. Furthermore, we actually attract circumstances that support our beliefs, and this seems less strange when we consider the research on attention and expectancy. Attention is the doorstep of perception, and all perception is subjective. To those who question that statement, physicist/psychologist William Powers asks whose retinas you would use in "objective" perception.

Human beings, along with all other living creatures, are goal-seeking. Our behavior is purposive and teleological (that's a ten-dollar word that means goal-seeking). It's the way our brains work. This concept is called *control theory* or *cybernetics* or *psycho-cybernetics*. The word *cybernetics* comes from the Greek word *kubernetes*, which means *steersman*. It's the same root as the Latin *gubernator*, which is where we get our word *governor*. *Cybernetics* was coined by the great mathematician Norbert Wiener, who saw a connection between the oscillation of a ship's steering mechanism and the difficulties of a human being afflicted with purpose tremor trying to thread a needle. The problem in both cases is excessive feedback. Cybernetics was Wiener's name for an interdisciplinary science that he saw as uniting all the other sciences with mathematics as a common language. What it says is that we set a goal or target and then steer for it with a series of course corrections, zig-zagging along like a torpedo toward its target. Like the torpedo, we learn from our mistakes and correct for them. We do this by using the feedback coming into our brains from the outside world.

Many people mistakenly believe that this is a mechanistic model that reduces human beings to machines. Not so. This model also describes the perceptual filters through which we view the world. Filters are part of the attention process. The tenth or highest of the filters—known as orders of perception—is *universal oneness*, which opens the door to many spiritual concepts. What drives or motivates the entire system is our basic needs: love, self-worth, fun, and freedom. The goals that we set are for things that we believe will meet these needs. Our goals can sometimes conflict with each other or with the goals of another person. Then too, we sometimes reach a goal and find that it did not meet our need; we were wrong about it. So as the old saying goes, be careful what you pray for (i.e., set as your goal), because you may get it! For example, we often try to meet our need for self-worth by being "right," so we make pessimistic predictions or concentrate on lack and limitation. And sure enough, we get it; we were right! The moral of that story is to put your attention on what you want.

Laboratory experiments have repeatedly demonstrated that thoughts of lack and limitation or sad, pessimistic thoughts have a negative effect on blood chemistry and overall physiology. Your brain becomes less able to think creatively, as capillaries shut down or constrict, and "I can't" becomes a self-fulfilling prophecy.

Physician Larry Dossey has done a meta-study (study of existing studies) on the efficacy of prayer, reported in his book *Healing Words*. More than half a hundred studies, some double-blind, support the efficacy of prayer to heal, the most efficacious form of prayer being some version of "Thy will be done" or a "let go and let God" approach, with "a sense of empathy, caring, and compassion." Once again, religion and science are being drawn together, whether they like it or not!

Get the Picture

Perhaps the single most effective technique you can use in the practice of the presence of God for practical purposes is visualization. This may or may not involve picturing your desired outcome, because some of us are more auditory or kinesthetic and may hear or feel our outcome. In any case, we create our desired outcome in our imagination in rich, sensory detail. Research again supports this notion by having demonstrated that the subconscious mind cannot distinguish between fact and vivid imagination. Success then can seem ordinary, an I-know-how-to-do-that feeling.

Visualization works best when the body is relaxed and the brain's hemispheres are synchronized. This means that the logical, linear left hemisphere has slowed down to mesh with the intuitive, holistic right hemisphere, creating a powerful synergy. Mysticism appears to be a right-hemisphere function. Psychiatrist Milton Erickson, who made hypnotism a respectable scientific discipline, believed that the subconscious mind was synonymous with the right (non-dominant) hemisphere of the brain. Is that how we become aware of our oneness with God?

Meditation also involves the relaxing of the body and the synchronization of the hemispheres. There are a zillion books and articles on how to meditate, both in and out of New Thought. Many people still think it sounds Eastern and weird, but psychiatrist Herbert Benson of Harvard has amassed a great deal of research to show the therapeutic value of meditation for the mind and the body. Meditation has strong ties to mysticism, and mysticism is found throughout the history of all religions, including Christianity and Judaism, even among some of the great intellectual lights such as St. Thomas Aquinas. Jesus was by any definition a mystic. But whether or not we experience God directly as a result of our meditation, a quiet mind and body are conducive to changing our thoughts and improving our physical health. "Be still, and know that I am God," says God in the Old Testament (Ps. 46:10). God is a pretty smart old bird.

New Thought and Economics

Prosperity consciousness has to do with believing in an abundant universe with plenty for all—and acting accordingly. There is much evidence to support this belief. See Julian Simon's *The*

Ultimate Resource for a refreshing look at the same statistics that many people use to predict gloom and doom.

Economics, which many people feel falls far short of being fully scientific, has strong psychological aspects. It is often called "the dismal science" because it is traditionally founded upon a belief in scarcity, in lack and limitation, in contraction rather than expansion. It deals with beliefs about supply and demand: if you believe that there is not enough of a commodity to meet demand, the price of that commodity goes up.

In New Thought we believe in an abundant universe in which a loving Father richly provides for his children. Lack and limitation are simply indications of our limited perspective. With an expanded perspective, we see that abundance is ours to claim. And now economist Paul Zane Pilzer has come up with an economics of abundance described in his book *Unlimited Wealth.* You've heard of someone trying to corner the market in, say, silver? Pilzer points out that markets have no corners. If a commodity such as silver becomes scarce, human ingenuity will uncover a new supply or come up with a substitute technology, which is exactly what happened with silver a few years ago. You don't worry about there not being enough of the pie to go around; you bake a bigger pie. But you don't do it with deception or greed, because deception and greed are really beliefs in lack and limitation, and it is done unto you as you believe.

If you give your attention to abundance and expect prosperity, you tend to get it. Consumer confidence, which economists talk about a lot and attempt to measure, has directly to do with what people expect. Do you want the economy to grow, to expand? Then don't think about or talk about lack and limitation. Put your attention on what you want. You can work to make things better without dwelling on what is wrong with them. As seventeenth-century Scottish Bishop Jeremy Taylor put it, "If thou has a bundle of thorns in thy lot, there is no need to sit down on it."

Still more help in developing an economics of abundance comes from Denise Breton and Christopher Largent, a husband-and-wife team of teacher-philosophers. In their book *The Soul of Economies—Spiritual Evolution Goes to the Marketplace,* they explain that economies are not determined by impersonal market forces; they are the product of people's philosophies. This is another way of saying that we get what we expect.

Breton and Largent urge us to "take the religions and philosophies of the world more into the marketplace" rather than have them remain "cut off from everyday affairs. We do academic or spiritual things, and then we do life." They point out our role in shaping economies: "Economies aren't out there happening to us. They are us." Then they add, "Doing something about economies starts with our minds. Changing *doing* without first changing *thinking* doesn't get us very far." (Does this sound familiar?) And they provide a tool kit of reliable methods for evolving philosophies.

The assumptions that we start with, say Breton and Largent, limit the strategies that are open to us. These strategies and assumptions shape our responses, which take us to our goals, which give directions to our assumptions, strategies, and responses.

Using the two different accounts of creation in Genesis as illustrations, Breton and Largent show how assumptions lead to economies of scarcity or abundance. Whole-seeking assumptions fuel the creative process, whereas assumptions that fragment hinder creativity and lead to a fight to survive. The Ten Commandments provide strategies for freedom. The Beatitudes provide responses that empower; and the Lord's Prayer, by turning us toward the whole, transforms us and gives us the purpose to evolve, which transforms economies.

If these folks aren't in New Thought, they ought to be.

Getting Through the Day

The number one New Thought suggestion for getting through the day is to change your mind and keep it changed. Like Brother Lawrence, New Thought teaches that our beliefs should help us get through the day. Since our experiences are derived from our beliefs, we might as well picture the best and expect the best, especially in view of the research on optimism and expectancy. Having survived the day, we need to take time to visualize and plan for the future that we want, that fulfills our mission in life; and take whatever steps we can to make it come about. The idea is not to keep living the same day over and over, but to visualize and plan for something better.

This reminds us of the story about the construction workers who ate lunch together. Every day one of them would open his lunch box and exclaim in disgust, "Peanut butter and jelly again!" Finally the other inquired, "Why don't you ask your wife to fix something else?" "Oh, I'm not married," was the reply. "I make my own lunch." All of us make our own lunch—with our thoughts.

No matter how limited we may feel at present, we can continue to visualize daily and be alert and ready for new opportunities, which have a way of suddenly appearing. If we are very clear about what we want, we will recognize such opportunities.

New Thoughter Joseph Murphy illustrates this well with an account of a scientist who was in a Russian concentration camp with no apparent hope of escape. He had seen pictures of Los Angeles, so every day and night he would picture himself driving along Wilshire Boulevard. One morning during roll call, the guard unexpectedly interrupted the count, and the scientist was able to step out of line and slip away without being missed. He made his way to Switzerland, where he met a couple from California who invited him to visit them there. He soon found himself being driven by their chauffeur along Wilshire Boulevard, just as he had pictured.

When we are embroiled in our problems, the hardest thing in the world is to picture what we want instead of stewing over— giving our attention to—what we don't want, which we thereby attract more of. There's nothing supernatural about it. Mysticism is helpful, but optional. What is *not* optional is the self-discipline necessary to back up our imagination with the will power to commit to and stay focused on what we want while taking whatever steps we are able to take to reach it. Those steps may include additional learnings, in or out of school, with perhaps some research in the local library, or seeking out a knowledgeable person to talk with. They may involve rethinking our attitudes and opinions about someone or something. They may involve breaking old habits, old patterns of doing things, and replacing them with new patterns. In any event, they mean *change*, and change is strange; otherwise it wouldn't be change. We have to be willing to put up with that strange feeling.

When problems have us discouraged, reading an inspirational book can help us raise our consciousness. New Thought literature runs the gamut from the sublime to the ridiculous, so you need to pick and choose what meets your needs. The words and actions of Jesus are our best role model, and symbolic interpretation of the Bible can make it relevant and meaningful for you. People have always had to scramble for a living, wrestle with health challenges, and struggle with relationships until they develop a prosperity consciousness, a habitually uplifted state of mind. You feel stressed? Read about St. Paul's shipwreck, or Daniel in the lions' den, as discussed by Emmet Fox. Now *there's* a stressful situation. Still, as Robert Schuller says, "Tough times never last, but tough people do." Old Daniel made out all right, as did Queen Esther in another Old Testament story involving even more stress than going to the boss to ask for a raise.

Robert Ringer, author of the much-misunderstood book *Winning Through Intimidation,* has a Theory of Sustenance of a Positive Attitude Through the Assumption of a Negative Result. This means preparing for long-term success by being prepared for short-term failure. Ringer points out that this works only if you are really prepared mentally to succeed and not merely seeking excuses for failure. You're only a failure if you say you are; otherwise, you just haven't succeeded yet. How many times did Edison fail to invent the light bulb before he finally succeeded? It was somewhere in the thousands of times. Control theory has a saying, "There is no failure, only feedback."

Charles Fillmore employed this nonnegative thinking when the sheriff came to repossess the printing press on which Fillmore had been unable to make payments. He said calmly to the sheriff, "I have a rich Father who is taking care of this." "Oh," said the sheriff, "in that case, we will give you a little more time." And of course, Fillmore's heavenly Father did come through, first with ideas, and eventually with lavish abundance, monetary and otherwise.

The self-disciplined, God-centered mind looks for the good in the midst of trouble and is therefore prepared to act when opportunity presents itself. You may not be able to prevent negative thoughts from coming into your mind, but you don't have to dwell on them. Emmet Fox likens them to a hot ash lighting on your sleeve. You can let it burn a hole or simply brush it off, and you certainly don't have to express negative thoughts aloud. It is literally true that words have power, and your brain hears what your mouth says. If you have to listen to yourself, you don't want to go around steeped in negativity; it's unhealthful. Remember the little prayer that goes, "Lord, help me make sure that my words are sweet and pleasant, for tomorrow I may have to eat them."

Even deep grief or catastrophe can be better dealt with by striving for an uplifted consciousness: "I will lift up mine eyes unto the hills, from whence cometh my help" (Ps. 121). We can also pray to be shown the good in any situation. This is especially helpful when no good at all seems apparent.

The disciplined mind is also disciplined in its dealings with others. Three of Covey's Seven Habits (see chapter 7) deal with interpersonal relationships: *Think win/win; Seek first to understand, then to be understood;* and *Synergize.* If we are all part of one good God, then there is good in each of us, even if it seems to be particularly well hidden in some. The most obnoxious or troublesome people in our lives are there to teach us something. When you have learned your lesson, you will find that either they change or they disappear from your life. You need to love them (remember, *love* means to wish someone well. *Well* in some cases might mean a brain transplant). We don't always know what is best for someone else.

Specific Techniques

New Thought is founded on the premise that we create our world with our thoughts (Process New Thought would say through our responses to God's initiatives in our lives, for those responses are largely experienced as thoughts). The only behaviors—and thoughts are behaviors—that we can change are our own. Changing our own thoughts changes at least slightly the background from which we and everything else emerge. Consequently, changing our thoughts really does change everything.

Specific thought-changing techniques include, in addition to Spiritual Mind Treatment and the Golden Key, any form of meditation along with visualization. Changing what you are doing with your body also helps you change your thoughts, especially when you go from inactivity to activity (overcomes depression), or from running around to resting (calms you down).

Changing our thoughts and keeping them changed requires the self-discipline of habitual practice of whatever techniques we select. This means that at least once a day and preferably oftener, we take the time to "sit in the silence," as Charles Fillmore put it, and become aware of God everywhere present. We can meditate, visualize, pray in conventional fashion, or walk in beautiful natural surroundings. But whatever we do, we get our thoughts off of our problems and onto God. Emmet Fox's technique called the Golden Key was simply that: stop thinking about the problem and instead mentally rehearse everything you know about God.

Science of Mind (Religious Science) founder Ernest Holmes developed a similar technique that he called Spiritual Mind Treatment, described in chapter 2. You can use it for yourself or others to get a new car, a job, a mate, a healing, new insight, or whatever else you desire. There are several variations, but it basically goes something like this: you focus your attention on God, feel your oneness with him/her, state your desired outcome *as if it had already occurred* (sometimes called "speaking your word"), give thanks that it is accomplished, and release any further thought or worry about the thing you are treating for, until time for your next treatment (let go and let God), if one is needed. Jesus regularly gave thanks in advance for his miracles.

Once into a calm, centered, uplifted state of consciousness, we can become aware of our mission in life, the fulfillment of which will bring us the greatest happiness. We can set goals and make plans to carry them out, guided by divine Wisdom. Emmet Fox defines Wisdom as a blend of Love and Intelligence, one of which without the other can get us into difficulties.

The practice of the presence of God for practical purposes empowers us. It teaches us that we are God individualized at the point where we are, all the love and power and abundance of God. We are not victims or worms of the dust or sinners, unless we say we are. We are cocreators with God, and our mission is to glorify God ("Inasmuch as ye have done it unto the least of my brethren, ye have done it unto me"—Matt. 25:40) by serving each other in ways suited to our particular talents and desires, which are God's perfect possibilities for us. To do this is to follow our bliss, to live in peace, harmony, joy, and abundance. Jesus said, "Give, and it shall be given unto you; good measure, pressed down, and shaken together, and running over" (Luke 6:38). To live this way is to be well; illness results when we are unhappy and out of balance, at odds with other people, or not making good use of our talents. Fear limits us; love empowers us. We are empowered when we change our thoughts and keep them changed, away from fear and separation and onto love and oneness. That can transform our lives: "Be ye transformed by the renewing of your mind" (Rom. 12:2).

Mildred Mann (1904–1971), founder of the Society of Pragmatic Mysticism, had a gift for putting things simply. In her *Become What You Believe* she defined treatment as

> nothing more than a change in your thoughts, at any given moment, from negative ideas to positive ones. [By turning one's attention to a favorite affirmation, a Bible text, or whatever] the conscious mind is forced to think in a new way. And according to the degree of concentrative ability the person has, it will begin to impress the subconscious mind [according to Process New Thought, a part of the past that is particularly relevant to you and has been built up of your past thoughts, attitudes, and actions] and change the emotion from fear to . . . peace. And then the outer picture, no matter what it is, will begin to change for the better.

Elsewhere in the book:

> The way is extremely simple, but definitely not easy. Still, it is no more difficult than learning to speak a foreign language, studying a new subject, or learning to do anything new. We train ourselves to think positively and constructively. Take any particular problem in your life, and face up to it. Don't deny that it exists, because it does, and has, through the sustenance your thought has given it. Now, you decide you are going to change your diet. You are going to put that problem on a starvation routine, by refusing to nourish it with thoughts which have fed it so far. You look through it; you realize it is but a shadow, because behind it lies the perfect pattern given you by your God. You make your mind dwell on that. When your thought slips back to the worry or fear patterns it has known, pull it back to positive thinking, and stick to it. This is the place where will power comes in, and it takes will power in the beginning.
>
> Remind yourself that you are a child of God. Within you is locked the perfection of Divinity [initial aim, in process terminology], and only you have the key to open it [to choose the perfect divine offer over the past]. No one can do that for you. You can only turn the key by turning your thought, and you can only keep the door open by keeping your thought turned in the direction of positive, constructive thinking.

Mildred Mann presents "Seven Steps in Demonstration":

> *Desire.* Get a strong enthusiasm for that which you want in your life, a real longing for something which is not there now.
>
> *Decision.* Know definitely what it is that you want, what it is that you want to do or have, and be willing to pay in spiritual values.

Ask. [When sure and enthusiastic] ask for it in simple, concise language. . . .

Believe [in the accomplishment with strong faith, consciously and subconsciously].

Work at it . . . a few minutes daily in seeing yourself in the finished picture. Never outline details, but rather see yourself enjoying the particular thing . . .

Feel gratitude. Always remember to say, "Thank you God," and begin to *feel* the gratitude in your heart. The most powerful prayer we can ever make is those three words, provided we really feel it.

Feel expectancy. Train yourself to live in a state of happy expectancy. . . . Act it—until it becomes part of you, as it must and will.

These are the seven steps. Follow them and they will bring you whatever it is that you need.

She summarizes:

Drop the problem, turn to God, and ask and claim your good. *Stay turned in that direction,* and you will have the secret of effective prayer.

She concludes the book with several "points to remember and think about":

YOU are Divine Spirit.
YOU are a child of God.
YOU have been given complete dominion over your life.
With God all things are possible.
You are never alone, for God is always with you.
Be positive in thought and word and deed.
Live up to the highest you know in all things.

See the Presence of God in your fellow man, particularly when you do not like him.

Give something of yourself in everything you do and to everyone you meet, particularly when you do not feel like it.

Meditate daily.

"In quietness and in confidence shall be your strength."—Isaiah 30:15

We'll let Jesus have the last word: "Fear not, little flock: for it is your Father's good pleasure to give you the kingdom" (Luke 12:32).

9

*

Sky-Blue Expressions:
An Affirmative Summary
of Who I Am

*W*hen William James wrote his chapter on mind-cure—mostly New Thought—in his classic study, *The Varieties of Religious Experience*, he appropriately titled the chapter "The Religion of Healthy-Mindedness." In it he guards against the view that "the happiness which a religious belief affords [is] a proof of its truth." But he takes note of "persons in every age, passionately flinging themselves upon their sense of the goodness of life, in spite of the hardships of their own condition, and in spite of the sinister theologies into which they may be born." James hopes

> that we all have some friend . . . whose soul is of this sky-blue tint, whose affinities rather with flowers and birds and all enhancing innocencies than with dark human passions, who can think no ill of man or God, and in whom religious gladness, being in possession from the outset, needs no deliverance from any antecedent burden.

Although the religion of healthy-mindedness may be "a deliberately optimistic scheme of life," much of it is spontaneous, and this may be found in its literature, some of which James found "so moon-struck with optimism and so vaguely expressed that an academically trained intellect finds it almost impossible to read it at all." But this may be at least partly because of the essentially mystical quality of many of New Thought's utterances. As James is famous for observing, one of the marks of mystical experience is its ineffability: "it defies expression . . . no adequate reports of its contents can be given in words." However any of this may be, it seems appropriate for us to conclude this book with some possibly moonstruck lines both expressive of the experiences underlying New Thought and consistent with the best attempts of philosophy to express the inexpressible.

These lines implement the teachings of this book, putting them into terms one can use as jumping-off points for meditation, for conveying truths that have roots deeper than any philosophy can state. These truths must be felt as well as understood.

I am love.

I am the great givingness of God centered in myself.
I am the awareness of generosity flowing forth to everyone and everything everywhere.
I am the abundance of God bursting forth unreservedly in my life and in all those with whom I have any contact (and in some degree that is everyone and everything).
I am a process through whom God enriches the universe.

I am joy.

I am the bubbling, laughing, smiling, charming spirit of all reality, coming forth through my awareness.
I am God's playmate, a small but indispensable source of God's joy. Even when I may not feel that I am a source of joy to myself, I have some awareness that my often stumbling growth is a source of satisfaction to God, even as a child's first efforts at walking are occasions for joy to the parent, who knows that great strides are in the offing.

I am God's unique project.

I am the bursting forth of goodness, of strength, of beauty, of humor, of cussedness, of ordinariness, of almost angelic balance, of splendid uniqueness.

I am an opportunity for God to accomplish something marvelous through me.

I let God do it!

I join wholeheartedly in the divine adventure of making something splendid that never has been before in the whole history of humanity.

I hardly can wait to see what God and I shall make!

I'm ready, God; let's go!

You lead the way and I'll do my best to embody you in the fullness of beautiful accomplishment.

I'll not waste time regretting that I didn't join in the fun more fully long ago.

I let that past be past, as I relish the present, in which we happily cocreate.

I am abundance.

I am the richness of the universe centered in myself, radiating forth to everyone.

I am the security that only awareness of unity with God can give.

I am that which cannot fade, which cannot disappear, which is ever new and abundant.

I am the certainty of divine assurance, the confidence of perfect power, perfect repose.

I am co-creator of my life.

Never do I go it alone. Never do I lack guidance. Never am I without perfect companionship—divine and, in whatever degree I choose it, human. I have never created on my own; it has always been co-creation with God, who gave the perfect ideas, the perfect possibilities even when I didn't listen. But now I KNOW; now I am open and aware that God and I work together; that neither God nor I can make this little bit of reality centered in me without the contribution of the other.

I am perfect peace.

I am so unshakably confident of the presence of the God who is perfect love that I have no fear, no trembling, no uncertainty that could undermine my confidence.

I am perfectly at ease. I know that I have given my life to God for perfect divine guidance and for loving acceptance.

I allow the alchemy of love to work its wondrous way in my life.

I give up all striving on my own, now that I know that God and I are partners, I the junior, happily cooperating with my Senior Partner.

I am endless enthusiasm.

I enthusiastically accept God's magnificent gift of fresh ideas every moment.

I know that the whole universe is present to me and providing all that I ever could need or want, as I choose it with God's guidance. I am eager to see what loving gift God will give me this moment as I give myself to God.

I am thankfulness unimaginable.

I am so grateful for God that I could shout, and in my own quiet—or boisterous, outrageous—way, I do!

I let my life shout my appreciation of God.

I don't need to talk about it, and I'm wise enough not to, except when people in words or other ways make it clear that they'd like to get more consciously into the divine act. Then I tell them what I can, but mostly I invite them to turn within and discover the glory that they have been hiding and maybe denying for decades.

As they grow, we grow together in the company of the smiling ones who blossom forth in common joy, yet unique in each expression of it.

I am free choice.

I realize that the essence of my life is freedom of choice.

I am not poured into anyone's mold.

I am not determined by the past.

I am free to choose from the alternatives provided by the pat-

tern of the past and by the perfect possibilities, the enlightened ideas, that God offers to me.

I am perfect paradox.

I am the silence that hollers.
I am the stillness that dances.
I am the beginning that is the end. I am the newness that is
   ancient.
I am the here that is everywhere.
I am eloquence without words.
I am the human that is divine.
I am the divine that is garbage.
I am the trees that walk.
I am the impossible possibilities.
I am something so great that it is nothing.
I am, so fully that I scarcely care whether I am at all.
I know without knowing.
I weep with neither sadness nor apparent joy.
I am I AM, yet ever i.

I am born anew.

Not born again, for I have never been before.
Yet I contain the ages.
All wisdom is mine.
But I know nothing other than the freshness of original birth.
I have all that I ever could want, even when I forget it.
Then I am new again in another first birth.
So it goes, moment by moment: a new self containing all my
   earlier selves, whom I love and lovingly escape from; I call
   them myself, yet I am privileged to transcend them.

I am me.

I note my immediate surroundings, and they are not-me. I become aware of my body, and I allow it to relax.

I become aware of my thoughts, and I allow them to slow and
then cease.

I become still and centered, waiting in the silence.

I begin to expand.

I become aware that I am one with the entire space I occupy.

I expand still further until I include the town, the state, the
continent.

I feel the oceans beating on my shores, the mountains rising in
my midst, the sky overhead.

I continue to expand until I include the planet, light on one
side, dark on the other.

I am the solar system, the galaxy, the universe.

I am one.

The Love that made me, is me, as me.

Somehow everything is as it should be.

Disasters, wars, cruelty, waste, disappointment, loss, are all part
of the same Whole as beauty, love, peace.

Chaos resolves into higher order.

The divine plan continues steadily, resolutely, dependably.

The darkness drops away, and all that remains is light and love.
All is well.

The Endless End

＊

Bibliography

Ahlstrom, Sydney E. *A Religious History of the American People*. New Haven, Conn. and London: Yale University Press, 1972.

Albanese, Catherine L. *Nature Religion in America from the Algonkian Indians to the New Age*. Chicago and London: University of Chicago Press, 1990.

Anderson, C. Alan. *A Guide to the Selection and Care of Your Personal God*. Canton, Mass.: Squantum Press, 1991.

———. *Healing Hypotheses: Horatio W. Dresser and the Philosophy of New Thought*. New York and London: Garland Publishing, 1993.

Andreas, Connirae, and Steve Andreas. *Change Your Mind—and Keep the Change*. Moab, Utah: Real People Press, 1987.

Bednarowski, Mary Farrell. *New Religions and the Theological Imagination in America*. Bloomington and Indianapolis: Indiana University Press, 1989.

Benson, Herbert. *Beyond the Relaxation Response*. New York: Berkley Books, 1984.

Bloom, Harold. *The American Religion: The Emergence of the Post-Christian Nation*. New York: Simon & Schuster, 1992.

Bowne, Borden Parker. *Personalism*. Boston and New York: Houghton Mifflin, 1908.

Braden, Charles S. *These Also Believe: A Study of Modern American Cults and Minority Religious Movements*. New York: Macmillan, 1949.

———. *Spirits in Rebellion: The Rise and Development of New Thought*. Dallas: Southern Methodist University Press, 1963.

Breton, Denise, and Christopher Largent. *The Soul of Economies: Spiritual Evolution Goes to the Marketplace*. Wilmington, Del.: Idea House Publishing, 1991.

Brightman, Edgar Sheffield. *A Philosophy of Religion*. New York: Prentice-Hall, 1940.

Bristol, Claude. *The Magic of Believing*. New York: Prentice-Hall, 1948.

Bruteau, Beatrice. *Radical Optimism: Rooting Ourselves in Reality*. New York: Crossroad Publishing, 1993.

Bucke, Richard Maurice. *Cosmic Consciousness: A Study in the Evolution of the Human Mind*. New York: E. P. Dutton and Co., 1901.

Butler, Jon. *Awash in a Sea of Faith: Christianizing the American People*. Cambridge, Mass. and London: Harvard University Press, 1990.

Christy, Arthur. *The Orient in American Transcendentalism: A Study of Emerson, Thoreau, and Alcott*. New York: Columbia University Press, 1932.

Clark, Mason Alonzo, ed. *The Healing Wisdom of Dr. P. P. Quimby.* Los Altos, Calif.: Frontal Lobe, 1982.

Cooper, John Charles. *Religion in the Age of Aquarius.* Philadelphia: Westminster Press, 1971.

Covey, Stephen R. *The Seven Habits of Highly Effective People: Restoring the Character Ethic.* New York: Simon & Schuster, 1989.

Csikszentmihalyi, Mihaly. *Flow: The Psychology of Optimal Experience.* New York: Harper & Row, Publishers, 1990.

D'Antonio, Michael. *Heaven on Earth: Dispatches from America's Spiritual Frontier.* New York: Crown Publishers, 1992.

Davis, Roy Eugene. *Miracle Man of Japan* [Taniguchi]. Lakemont, Ga.: CSA Press, 1970.

DeChant, Dell. "Taproots of the New: New Thought and the New Age." *The Quest* 4 (Winter 1991), 68–77.

Dictionary of Pentecostal and Charismatic Movements. Stanley M. Burgess and Gary B. McGee, eds.; Patrick H. Alexander, assoc. ed. Grand Rapids, Mich.: Zondervan Publishing, 1988. See esp. Introduction; P. G. Chappell, "Healing Movements"; P. D. Hocken, "Charismatic Movements."

Dossey, Larry. *Healing Words: The Power of Prayer and the Practice of Medicine.* San Francisco: HarperCollins, 1993.

Dresser, Horatio W. *A History of the New Thought Movement.* New York: Thomas Y. Crowell, 1919.

Dresser, Horatio W., ed. *The Spirit of the New Thought.* New York: Thomas Y. Crowell, 1917.

———. *The Quimby Manuscripts.* New York: Thomas Y. Crowell, 1921.

Elder, Dorothy. *From Metaphysical to Mystical.* Denver: Doriel Publishing, 1992.

The Encyclopedia of Religion. Mircea Eliade, ed., 16 vols. New York: Macmillan Publishing, 1987.

Evans, Warren Felt. *The Mental Cure.* Boston: H. H. & T. W. Carter & Co., 1869.

———. *The Divine Law of Cure.* Boston: H. H. Carter & Co., 1881.

Ferguson, Marilyn. *The Aquarian Conspiracy* (rev. ed.). Los Angeles: J. P. Tarcher, 1987.

Fillmore, Charles. *Metaphysical Bible Dictionary.* Unity Village, Mo.: Unity School of Christianity, 1931.

———. *The Revealing Word.* Unity Village, Mo.: Unity School of Christianity, 1959.

Foundation for Inner Peace. *A Course in Miracles,* combined volume, 2d ed. Glen Ellen, Calif.: Foundation for Inner Peace, 1992. (Original three volumes published in 1976.)

Fowler, James W. *Stages of Faith: The Psychology of Human Development and the Quest for Meaning.* San Francisco: Harper & Row, 1981.

Fox, Emmet. *The Sermon on the Mount.* New York: Harper & Brothers, 1934.

———. *Alter Your Life.* New York: Harper & Brothers, 1950.

Gallup, George, Jr. and Jim Castelli. *The People's Religion: American Faith in the 90's.* New York: Macmillan Publishing, 1989.

George, Carol V. R. *God's Salesman: Norman Vincent Peale and the Power of Positive Thinking.* New York: Oxford University Press, 1993.

Givens, Charles. *Wealth Without Risk.* New York: Simon & Schuster, 1991.

Glasser, William. *Stations of the Mind.* New York: Harper & Row, 1981.

Greven, Philip. *The Protestant Temperament: Patterns of Child-Rearing, Religious Experience, and the Self in Early America.* New York: Alfred A. Knopf, 1977.

Griffin, David Ray, and Huston Smith. *Primordial Truth and Postmodern Theology.* Albany: State University of New York Press, 1989.

Hartshorne, Charles. *The Logic of Perfection and Other Essays in Neoclassical Metaphysics.* La Salle, Ill.: Open Court Publishing, 1962.

———. *Insights and Oversights of Great Thinkers: An Evaluation of Western Philosophy.* Albany, N.Y.: State University of New York Press, 1983.

———. *Omnipotence and Other Theological Mistakes.* Albany, N.Y.: State University of New York Press, 1984.

Hartshorne, Charles and William L. Reese, eds. *Philosophers Speak of God.* Chicago: University of Chicago Press, 1953.

Hatch, Nathan O. *The Democratization of American Christianity.* New Haven, Conn. and London: Yale University Press, 1989.

Hill, Napoleon. *Think and Grow Rich.* New York: Fawcett-Crest, 1960.

Holmes, Ernest. *New Thought Terms and Their Meanings: A Dictionary of the Terms and Phrases Commonly Used in Metaphysical and Psychological Study.* New York: Dodd, Mead & Co., 1942. (Published in modified form as *A Dictionary of New Thought Terms* in 1991 by DeVorss & Co., Marina del Rey, Calif.)

Holmes, Ernest, and Maud Allison Lathem, eds. *Mind Remakes Your World.* New York: Dodd, Mead & Co., 1941.

Huber, Richard M. *The American Idea of Success.* New York: McGraw-Hill, 1971.

Hudson, Thomson Jay. *The Law of Psychic Phenomena: A Working Hypothesis for the Systematic Study of Hypnotism, Spiritism, Mental Therapeutics, Etc.* Chicago: A. C. McClurg & Co., 1893.

Introduction to Seicho-No-Ie. Published by Seicho-No-Ie, probably from its North American Missionary Headquarters, 14527 South Vermont Ave., Gardena, Calif. 90247. (10 pp. inside paper covers.)

James, William. *The Varieties of Religious Experience.* New York: Longmans, Green & Co., 1902.

Judah, J. Stillson. *The History and Philosophy of the Metaphysical Movements in America.* Philadelphia: Westminster Press, 1967.

Katz, Steven, ed. *Mysticism and Philosophical Analysis.* New York: Oxford University Press, 1978.

Kaufman, Barry Neil. *Son-Rise.* New York: Harper & Row, 1976.

———. *Happiness Is a Choice.* New York: Fawcett-Columbine, 1991.

Knudson, Albert C. *The Doctrine of God.* New York: Abingdon Press, 1930.

Kosmin, Barry A., and Seymour P. Lachman. *One Nation Under God: Religion in Contemporary American Society.* New York: Harmony Books, 1993.

Kuhn, Thomas S. *The Structure of Scientific Revolutions.* Chicago: University of Chicago Press, 1970.

Lee, Philip J. *Against the Protestant Gnostics.* New York and Oxford: Oxford University Press, 1987.

Leonard, George. *Mastery.* New York: Penguin/Plume, 1991.

Lewis, James R., and J. Gordon Melton, eds. *Perspectives on the New Age.* Albany, N.Y.: State University of New York Press, 1992.

Mann, Mildred. *Become What You Believe.* New York: privately published c. 1955.

(Now available from Society of Pragmatic Mysticism, RR #1, Box 800, Pawlet, Vt. 05761.)

Matlin, M., and D. Stang. *The Pollyanna Principle.* Cambridge, Mass.: Schenkman Publishing, 1978.

McLaughlin, Corinne, and Gordon Davidson. *Spiritual Politics: Changing the World from the Inside Out.* New York: Ballantine Books, 1994.

Melton, J. Gordon. *The Encyclopedia of American Religions.* 3d ed. Detroit: Gale Research, 1989.

———. Jerome Clark, and Aidan Kelly. *New Age Almanac.* Detroit: Visible Ink Press (division of Gale Research, 1991).

Meyer, Donald. *The Positive Thinkers: Popular Religious Psychology from Mary Baker Eddy to Norman Vincent Peale and Ronald Reagan.* Revised ed. Middletown, Conn.: Wesleyan University Press, 1988.

Morris, Tom [Thomas V.]. *True Success: A New Philosophy of Excellence.* New York: G. P. Putnam's Sons, 1994.

Murphy, Joseph. *The Power of the Subconscious Mind.* Englewood Cliffs, N.J.: Prentice-Hall, 1963.

Naisbitt, John, and Patricia Aburdene. *Megatrends 2000: Ten New Directions for the 1990s.* New York: William Morrow and Co., 1990.

Neville, Robert Cummings. *The Highroad Around Modernism.* Albany, N.Y.: State University of New York Press, 1992.

Odin, Steve. *Process Metaphysics and Hua-Yen Buddhism: A Critical Study of Cumulative Penetration vs. Interpenetration.* Albany, N.Y.: State University of New York Press, 1982.

Otto, Rudolf. *The Idea of the Holy: An inquiry into the non-rational factor in the idea of the divine and its relation to the rational.* Trans. John W. Harvey. New York: Oxford University Press, 1926.

Paden, William E. *Religious Worlds.* Boston: Beacon Press, 1988.

Peale, Norman Vincent. *The Power of Positive Thinking.* New York: Prentice-Hall, 1952.

Peck, M. Scott. *Further Along the Road Less Traveled: The Unending Journey Toward Spiritual Growth.* New York: Simon & Schuster, 1993.

Pilzer, Paul Zane. *Unlimited Wealth.* New York: Crown Publishers, 1990.

Ponder, Catherine. *The Dynamic Laws of Prosperity.* Englewood Cliffs, N.J.: Prentice-Hall, 1962.

———. *The Prosperity Secret of the Ages.* Englewood Cliffs, N.J.: Prentice-Hall, 1964.

Quebedeaux, Richard. *By What Authority: The Rise of Personality Cults in American Christianity.* San Francisco: Harper & Row, 1982.

Ringer, Robert. *Winning Through Intimidation.* Los Angeles: Los Angeles Book Publishers Co., 1974.

Robbins, Anthony. *Awaken the Giant Within.* New York: Summit Books, 1991.

Schneider, Louis, and Sanford M. Dornbusch. *Popular Religion: Inspirational Books in America.* Chicago: University of Chicago Press, 1958.

Seale, Ervin. *Mingling Minds: Some Commentary on the Philosophy and Practice of Phineas Parkhurst Quimby.* Linden, N.J.: Tide Press, 1986.

Seale, Ervin, ed. *Phineas Parkhurst Quimby: The Complete Writings.* 3 vols. Marina Del Rey, Calif.: DeVorss & Co., 1988.

Seligman, Martin E. P. *Learned Optimism*. New York: Alfred A. Knopf, 1991.

Sia, Santiago. *God in Process Thought*. Dordrecht, Netherlands: Martinus Nijhoff Publishers, 1985.

Simon, Julian. *The Ultimate Resource*. Princeton, N.J.: Princeton University Press, 1981.

Sinetar, Marsha. *Do What You Love, The Money Will Follow*. New York: Dell Publishing, 1987.

Smith, Huston. *Beyond the Post-Modern Mind* (updated and revised ed.) Wheaton, Ill.: Theosophical Publishing House, 1989.

Tillich, Paul. *Dynamics of Faith*. New York: Harper, 1957.

———. *Theology of Culture*. New York: Oxford University Press, 1959.

Underhill, Evelyn. *Mysticism*. New York: E. P. Dutton & Co., 1911.

———. *Practical Mysticism*. New York: E. P. Dutton &. Co., 1915.

Whitehead, Alfred North. *Process and Reality: An Essay in Cosmology*. New York: Macmillan, 1929.

———. *Modes of Thought*. New York: Macmillan, 1938.

Wilber, Ken. *Eye to Eye: The Quest for the New Paradigm*. Expanded ed. Boston: Shambhala Publications, 1990.

Wilcox, Ella Wheeler. *The Heart of New Thought*. Chicago: Psychic Research Co., 1902.

Index